HOW TO PRICE EFFECTIVELY

EFFECTIVELY

A GUIDE FOR MANAGERS AND
ENTREPRENEURS

UTPAL DHOLAKIA

Contents

The greatest gift is the power to estimate correctly the value of things.

—Le Rochefoucauld

[1]

THE PURPOSE OF THIS BOOK

Pricing is the moment of truth—all of marketing comes to focus in the pricing decision. – E. Raymond Corey

I have taught a graduate-level business school course on pricing strategy for well over a decade at Rice University. During this time, I have also worked with dozens of companies, from single-person startups to some of the largest corporations in the world on pricing issues. I have helped make pricing decisions for everything, from industrial machinery costing millions of dollars to a line of craft beer, from a medical test to detect sexually transmitted diseases to an upscale nightclub. Throughout, it has surprised me just how much otherwise smart, knowledgeable, and confident managers and entrepreneurs are intimidated when it comes to making pricing decisions, and how often they avoid thinking deeply about pricing issues.

1

The Significance of Pricing Decisions

Pricing decisions are among the most important and impactful business decisions that a manager can make. They are arguably one of the few decisions that affect a company's revenues directly. Paradoxically, setting a price or changing one is also among the easiest things to do today. One push of a computer key, one revised number in a spreadsheet, or a new price label affixed to a product, and the pricing is done.

When made thoughtfully, using a structured process that takes the relevant factors into account, and when executed competently at the company's frontlines, pricing decisions can propel the company on a path of sustained differentiation, rapid growth, healthy profits, satisfied customers, and engaged employees. However, if pricing is done haphazardly, using old traditions without sound reasoning, or with cookie-cutter methods that only pay attention to the company's costs or the prices of one particular competitor, it can lead to lost opportunity. Defective pricing can fritter away a company's competitive advantage, leaving customers irate, employees confused, and sales in a freefall. Simply put, pricing decisions are "make or break" decisions.

What is more, pricing decisions are recurrent. Through both lean and prosperous periods, whether introducing an exciting new product[1] or only trying to sell the same old products, whether it is in the driver's seat or struggling to catch up with its competitors, every company must periodically set prices for new products and change prices for existing products. Each new day brings the opportunity to erase past pricing mistakes and to turn the page over. On the flip side, past pricing performance is not indicative of future success. Every new pricing decision is fraught with risk. This is why using a structured and consistent process is invaluable.

Pricing decisions are almost never discipline-specific, nor are they made and executed in a silo. The marketing, sales, strategy, operations, and accounting functions each play a significant role in the success of a company's pricing strategy. Pricing choices are grounded in the company's culture, and influenced by its historical thinking. For many managers, the philosophy of: "Let's not rock the boat, this is how we priced our products last year, and everything seemed fine. So let's do it the same way again this year" seems like a sensible way to make pricing decisions.

In fact, the most common problem I encounter when working with established companies is how to pull them away from tradition-bound pricing methods to which they have become accustomed. In most cases, this means focusing almost entirely on covering costs. The company ignores other relevant factors such as its overall marketing strategy and the value proposition it wants to deliver to customers, the economic value customers place on its products, and the reference prices they use for comparison, including the prices of major competitors.

The challenge is different but equally significant for startups. Most startup founders give little thought to pricing questions, and tend to be unduly swayed by industry norms. They imitate the pricing approach of peer companies, or of exciting startups that have gone on to become wildly successful, without carefully thinking about whether such pricing models make sense for their new business.

What is a good pricing decision? What factors should you consider and what methods should you use when making pricing decisions? Is charging revenue-maximizing prices (assuming you can figure out how to do this) the best thing to do? Alternatively, is the price that maximizes the company's profit the best one? Can you do both, maximize revenue and profit simultaneously? Which factors should you consider when setting and changing prices? How can you earn the prices you have set? How will you know that you have made the right pricing decision and that your pricing strategy is working? What performance measures should you track to evaluate your pricing? What are the pricing best practices in business and consumer markets? These questions animate this book. They form the foundation to build an effective pricing strategy for your organization.

THE VALUE PRICING FRAMEWORK

To answer these questions, this book will provide an in-depth discussion and understanding of the *value pricing framework* that I have developed over the past decade. The *value pricing framework* is a structured, versatile, and comprehensive method for making good pricing decisions and executing them. It weaves together the latest thinking from academic research journals, proven best practices from the leading pricing experts, and ideas from other fields such as medical decision making, consumer behavior, and organizational psychology. It is strategic, structured, multi-faceted, and its use will instill confidence in your company's products, and satisfaction with the price and the pricing process in your employees and customers. The *value pricing framework* has been extensively road-tested. Over the past decade, it has been employed in many different contexts to tackle a variety of pricing issues successfully. It is applicable whether you work for an established company or if you are about to launch a brand new startup.

Even when managers or entrepreneurs do not know of it, or call it as such, many of them employ parts of this framework in a piecemeal way. In this book, my goal is to formalize this structured method, by describing, explaining, and applying each part of it in depth. After reading this book, you should have a clear understanding of what a good pricing decision is, which factors you should consider when making one, the role played by each factor, how they work together, the importance of price execution, and how to evaluate the success of pricing decisions. You will also be introduced to a set of useful and straightforward tools to implement the *value pricing framework*, and study many examples and company case studies that illustrate its nuances. The purpose of this book is to provide you with a comprehensive, practical guide to making, executing, and evaluating pricing decisions.

Whether you are a manager of marketing, sales, operations, accounting, or strategy functions, a consultant, or an entrepreneur, if you play a role in your company's or your client's pricing activities, you will find the material covered in this book to be useful. When you have finished reading it, I hope the building blocks of the *value pricing framework* and the philosophy behind it will be part of your everyday vocabulary and mindset. Each time you encounter an opportunity to evaluate, change, or realize your company's prices, you should be able to rely on this framework to make good pricing decisions.

WHY WRITE THIS BOOK?

Over the years, my students, clients, and others have asked me to recommend pricing books on many occasions. There are dozens of pricing books out there, and many of them are excellent and are referenced in this book. However, despite much searching, I could not find a single book that covered every component of the *value pricing framework* in a structured way. I decided to write this book as a practical guide that includes all relevant information needed to think about pricing issues and make effective pricing decisions.

I have observed two common things about pricing books. First, some tend to be long-winded, stretching out ideas that could be explained succinctly. Readers have to skim through a lot of filler to reach the substance. Others tend to be specialized, covering a narrow topic in comprehensive detail for a pricing expert. However, neither type of book provides a systematic way to think about pricing issues for readers who may not know much about it, and who want to apply it to their business.

The second odd and surprising thing about pricing books is their price. When seen through my open-source inspired way of thinking, most pricing books seem to have very high prices that maximize profit per copy but do not provide broad access. To be fair, authors have little control over their book's price. It is often the publisher and the retailer that determine the book's price.

In writing this book, I wanted to avoid the things I dislike about other pricing books. I have written this book for managers and entrepreneurs who want a structured method to think about pricing issues for their company or startup. The book is organized around the *value pricing framework*. In the chapters that follow, I describe the foundations of this framework in Chapters 2 and 3. After that, I cover one major component of the framework in each chapter, from Chapters 4 to 9. In each chapter, I get to the core idea and insights about it quickly, but with sufficient discussion and illustration through examples and case studies so that they are clear, and you can apply them to your business. The final two chapters, 10 and 11, are about using the *value pricing framework* in business and consumer markets, respectively. This book is full of practical tools and ideas that you can use right away.

Effective pricing forms the backbone of a successful marketing strategy and holds the key to every organization's long-term financial performance. My hope is that by understanding and using the concepts described in the *value pricing framework*, you will be able to make effective pricing decisions and realize your asked-for prices every time.

[2]

WHAT IS A GOOD PRICING DECISION?

It's not hard to make decisions when you know what your values are. – Roy Disney

Managers today have an almost unlimited choice of marketing levers to improve their firm's bottom-line. They can hire more frontline employees to upgrade service quality and provide a better customer experience. They can refresh the brand logo and tagline to create a more contemporary image. They can introduce a new distribution channel and gain access to new customers. If they have a large advertising budget at their disposal, they may even consider running a television advertisement during the Super Bowl or the Oscars to generate brand exposure and publicity. When used correctly, each of these marketing levers will increase the company's sales and profit.

PRICING IS THE MOST POWERFUL PROFIT LEVER

Of all marketing levers, however, an effective pricing strategy can do more for the company's bottom-line than any other lever. Over the years, many studies have repeatedly shown that, when compared to cutting costs, increasing sales, or spending more on advertising and publicity, raising prices is a more powerful profit lever.

The most well-known and widely-cited of these studies is the McKinsey Global 1200 pricing study. When they compiled and analyzed the income statements of the world's 1,200 largest firms, McKinsey consultants Walter Baker, Michael Marn, and Craig Zawada found that increasing prices by just 1% (without changing cost inputs or sales) would raise the average company's operating profit by 8.7%. The similar effects of changing sales (+2.8% increase in profit), variable costs (+5.9%) and fixed costs (+1.8%) for these companies were all considerably smaller. The consultants concluded, "Pricing is far and away the most powerful profit lever that a company can influence." Even small increases in prices lead to an amplified profit growth for the organization[1].

Using business performance data from 2012, pricing expert Hermann Simon pointed out that if telecom provider Verizon had been able to increase its prices by just 2% that year without losing any sales, it would have tripled its profit. Energy multinational BP would have increased its profits by 50% with a similar price increase[2]. Pricing consultant Rafi Mohammed offered an equally compelling thought experiment to demonstrate the strong profit impact of pricing decisions. According to him, if

warehouse chain Costco were to raise the price of its famous re-
cession and inflation-proof hot dog and soda combo from $1.50
by just two pennies to $1.52 in its stores, and then make the same
pricing move on its other products, its operating profit would
shoot up by 48%[3]! These different numerical examples and
thought experiments all make the same essential point: ***A small
increase in prices while maintaining the firm's sales and cost levels
generates a significant boost to its profit.***

Of course, the opposite is also true. Reducing prices by even a
little without gaining sufficient incremental sales will devastate
the company's profits. Do you know the profit impact of price
changes for your business? A good starting point for implementing the *value pricing framework* in your company is to find the
answer. Specifically, once you calculate the percentage by which
your company's profit will increase if you can increase prices by
just 2% without losing any sales, this value, whatever it is, will
provide you and your colleagues with the motivation to take pricing seriously, and make pricing decisions thoughtfully. Here is
my prediction: the lower your company's profit margin is the
stronger will be the impact of the pricing lever on your company's profit. As you will see throughout this book, there are many
ways to earn a price increase of 2%, and, counter-intuitively,
some of them do not involve raising asked-for prices.

PRICING PERFORMANCE IMPROVEMENT IS A SIGNIFICANT OPPORTUNITY

Even though pricing decisions are among the most important
decisions any business can make, far too many companies do not
pay sufficient attention to them. They price their products too

high or too low, change prices too often, run far too many promotions, give customers deeper discounts than necessary, or fail at price execution. The struggle of airplane manufacturers like Boeing and Airbus with pricing is typical of the price execution challenge[4]. Year after year, these firms raise their catalog prices when they introduce new or updated airplanes. And like clockwork, their customers, the major airlines, play hardball. They negotiate prices down, nullifying the asked-for price increases. The increase in catalog prices is meaningless. The actual prices airlines have paid for new airplane purchases have not budged in years.

Such a thrust and parry dynamic between companies trying to raise prices and customers talking them down highlights the fact that simply increasing prices is not enough. An important part of an effective pricing strategy is to follow through and get customers to pay the asking price.

Many organizations lack focus in pricing decisions because setting or changing prices is an intimidating endeavor. To many managers, a pricing decision feels like a challenging and consequential decision to make. Out of fear they will get it wrong, they put it off or pass it to someone else. Even when they are decisive, managers use incomplete information or focus on the wrong variables because they do not know which factors are important and need to be considered, and which ones can be safely ignored. Finally, they lack visibility into how well they are executing, and which measures they should track to evaluate their pricing.

THE PUZZLING CASE OF THE SUCCESSFUL HANDBAG MAKER

A few years ago, I worked with an entrepreneur who had grown her company from nothing to over $1 million in sales in less than two years. She is a creative and skilled craftswoman and a top-notch designer. At the time, the only products she sold were an extremely popular line of leather handbags. Every time she participated in a trunk show at a boutique store, she sold out of her bags within hours. She could not produce her handbags fast enough. On the surface, it seemed that she had a winning product and a customer-focused marketing strategy. Her customers loved her products, and her sales were growing briskly, constrained only by the growth of the manufacturing capacity.

However, her bank accounts told an entirely different story. In truth, she was barely breaking even. When we talked through her pricing process and considered how she made pricing decisions, it turned out the entrepreneur did not know how much money it cost her to make a leather handbag. Nor did she fully appreciate just how much her customers liked her bags, or recognize that they were willing to pay considerably more than she was asking. In effect, she had priced her products 20-30% lower than what they should have been. Her customers were very happy and lined up to buy the handbags at trunk shows. Although she was nervous, the entrepreneur raised prices substantially to align them with the valuation of customers and with the image she wanted her brand to portray. Three months after the price increase, handbag sales remained steady, cash flow and profits had soared, and the business was back on track.

It is amazing how often entrepreneurs, managers, and company owners approach pricing decisions as an afterthought, or not at all. They put tremendous amounts of personal effort, time, and money into designing new products, branding, customer service, and finding new distribution channels, but very few, if any, of these resources into making pricing decisions.

This is a core message of this book.

> **Pricing decisions are necessary for your company's success. Pay attention to them, and spend significant time and effort in thinking about your company's pricing strategy. Collect relevant data about all decision inputs and analyze it carefully. Make your pricing decisions in a structured, methodical, and consistent way.**

Across different industries, another common theme is that managers are reticent about high prices. They would rather take the path of least resistance and keep prices low or offer incentives. They would rather let customers enjoy great deals by paying far lower prices than the products deserve or what they are willing to pay, even if this means that the company's future hangs in the balance.

Another important takeaway from this book is this:

> **A high price is a badge of your product's superior quality. The high price is a signifier conveying positive qualities that your customers value such as reliability, innovativeness, comfort, convenience, and status that strengthens your brand, supplies pride and confidence to your employees and builds trust with your customers. When you make high-quality products and services, high prices are a strength, and low prices are a hindrance for marketing them, and for increasing sales and profit.**

WHAT IS A GOOD PRICING DECISION?

The *value pricing framework* is built on this foundational question. On the surface, the answer may seem obvious to managers and entrepreneurs. However, in reality, it is deceptively difficult[5]. When managers are asked what they consider good pricing decisions, they will reflexively assert that good pricing decisions are ones that "maximize the company's sales" or those that "maximize the company's profit." Less often, they will say that a good pricing decision is one that delivers superior customer value or helps to build and strengthen customer relationships. When the pricing environment is challenging, they may say that a good pricing decision is one that allows the company to survive severe conditions and live to fight another day. These answers all confuse the process of making pricing decisions with their outcomes. More problematically, the responses make the mistake of focusing exclusively on the results and ignoring the decision-making process entirely.

When making a pricing decision (or any business decision for that matter), the manager decides at one point in time, and the results of the decision occurs afterward, sometimes weeks or months later. In fact, for most pricing decisions, the outcomes occur over an indeterminate length of time. Consider, for instance, the boost in sales that occurs when a grocery store runs a 72-hour promotion on some of its products. A portion of the sales increase comes from customers who buy and use more of the promoted products, but many sales during the promotion are made to shoppers who are only stocking up because the items they regularly purchase and use are on sale[6]. In the case of these customers, the 72-hour promotion is "stealing" from full-priced future sales. It is difficult to pinpoint exactly how much of the grocery store's sales increase is real, and how much is taken from future sales. The promotion's success cannot be accurately ascertained by measuring sales or even calculating the change in sales.

What is more, pricing decisions do not occur in a vacuum. After a decision is made, and before its outcomes can be ascertained, factors outside the manager's or the firm's control may exert strong influence. Such impacts can be positive or negative and may have little to do with pricing. To understand this important point, let us consider two cases briefly. The first one describes the traumatic experience of the famous Texas-based ice cream maker, Blue Bell Creameries. The second case is about the good fortune of Spin Master, the toy company that made the Hatchimals, 2016's hottest toy.

THE BLUE BELL CREAMERIES PRODUCT RECALL

Imagine it is March 2015 and you are the pricing manager at Blue Bell Creameries. You have made the decision to raise your ice cream's prices by 10% for the convenience store channel through the summer season. You want to increase the profit margin from this channel because convenience store shoppers buy ice cream on impulse and are less price sensitive.

A similar seasonal price increase was very successful last year. You have every expectation that sales will be stable and profits will rise during the hot Texas summer months. You feel very comfortable with your decision. You have made it thoughtfully, in a systematic way, after considering the relevant factors such as your costs, competitors' prices, how convenience store customers buy ice cream, how much they love your brand and your company's value proposition.

Fast forward to two months later. Calamity has struck. Compared to last year, your company's ice cream sales in Texas are down by more than 70%. The drop in profits is even greater. The main reason has nothing to do with prices. Your company, Blue Bell, had to recall all ice cream products because of a listeria outbreak in its manufacturing facility[7]. You are devastated. Full of regret, the big question in your mind is, "Would the results be any better if we had maintained or lowered prices in convenience stores instead of increasing them? Did I make a bad pricing decision?"

PRICING THE HATCHIMALS, THE HOTTEST TOY OF 2016

Imagine it is July 2016, and you are the pricing manager at Spin Master, the Canadian toy company. Utilizing the *value pricing framework*, you have just gone through a structured process to price your new toy, called the Hatchimals[8]. Hatchimals, which are interactive fuzzy toy creatures that hatch out of an egg after lots of coaxing, will be launched globally in early October, just in time for the 2016 holiday shopping season. Based on careful analysis of costs, customers' reference prices, and your firm's distribution and branding strategies, you have settled on a suggested retail price of $60 for each Hatchimal.

Five months pass, and it is New Year's Day 2017. Thanks to constant media coverage and social media buzz, Hatchimals have been a smashing success. In fact, they were the "hot toy" of the holiday season all over the world. Shoppers were so desperate to get their hands on one, they lined up outside Toys "R" Us,

Walmart, and Target stores for hours. As soon as a new shipment of Hatchimals arrived, they sold out within minutes. Opportunistic consumers resold these toys on eBay, where the average prices for a Hatchimal rose to $143[9]. Hundreds of amateur sellers and many professionals made more money by reselling your toy in the secondary market than your company did. You shake your head sadly and wonder, "Was my pricing decision a bad one? Should I have set the Hatchimals' price higher than $60?"

THE DISTINCTION BETWEEN THE PRICING DECISION PROCESS AND PRICING OUTCOMES

In both these hypothetical scenarios, the answer to whether the pricing decision made was a good one or bad one was complicated by the fact that unforeseen external circumstances intervened to affect the outcomes. For Blue Bell, the ice cream's recall negated any potential benefits of increasing prices. For Spin Master, the unexpected media-driven success led to massive product demand and scarcity throughout the holiday shopping season and drove up prices in the secondary market. In both cases, there was a mismatch between the thoughtful, structured process used to make the pricing decision and the outcomes that followed. Still, the answer in both cases is that, despite the second-guessing, the managers made good pricing decisions.

Whether it is the military, medicine, or industry, decision-making experts have warned against relying on outcomes when evaluating a decision's quality and judging whether the decision was a good one. In medical decision making, for instance, physicians are taught the concept of making an "informed decision" when helping patients to choose between different treatment options. An informed medical decision is one where all the available information about the various options is gathered and weighted, and the final choice includes a consideration of the patient's and the physician's values[10]. In other words, a good medical decision has two properties: (1) the patient has considered all relevant factors, and gathered and utilized appropriate information about each course of action, and (2) the choice reflects the decision maker's core values.

Notice that in this definition of an informed decision, nothing is said about the patient's health outcomes. This omission acknowledges that numerous factors are outside the patient's and the physician's control, and have nothing to do with the decision process, that can still affect the patient's health outcome. Under these circumstances, the best that the patient and physician can do is put their heads together and make an informed decision, and then implement it. The outcomes will take care of themselves. This is an imperative point that is equally valid for pricing decisions and is a core aspect of what we consider a good pricing decision. In the *value pricing framework*:

> **A good pricing decision is one that is made deliberately and thoughtfully, considers all relevant factors—costs, customer value, reference prices, and the value proposition, is based on the company's business philosophy & values, and is explained clearly to customers and to employees involved in implementing it.**

In other words, a good pricing decision uses a structured, information-based process consistently. Having a rigorous process that is used consistently is essential because most pricing decisions take place within an uncertain, volatile, and intensely competitive business environment. Part of what makes the decision a good one is its comprehensive and unambiguous communication to customers and the frontline employees responsible for implementing it.

THE FOUR PILLARS OF PRICING

When making pricing decisions with a structured process, you should consider four main factors. We will call these factors the "four pillars of pricing" because each one provides an essential input for effective pricing decisions. In this chapter, we will briefly introduce the four pillars, and consider them in detail later in this book. The four pillars of pricing are:

Figure 2.1 The four pillars of pricing

Costs. Costs are the most commonly recognized factor in a pricing strategy and usually set the floor on prices. A majority of prices are set based only, or mainly, using costs. In pricing, costs are separated into incremental costs that are relevant to the pricing decision and need to be considered carefully, and non-incremental or irrelevant costs, that should be ignored. Understanding each of these costs and how they will change with the pricing decision is a critical task. In addition to setting the floor on prices, costs can also serve as the centerpiece of the company's marketing strategy. We will discuss these roles played by costs in the *value pricing framework* in Chapter 4.

Customer value. The second pillar of pricing is customer value. It is the total amount of money that the customer is willing to pay for functional and hedonic benefits received from the product. The value grid, discussed in detail later on, provides a straightforward and effective method of understanding how the product's features translate into customer benefits, which in turn lead to the customer's willingness to pay. Customer value usually sets the ceiling or the highest possible price that can be charged for the product. We will consider the roles of customer value in Chapter 5.

Reference prices. Customers rarely make purchase decisions or evaluate prices in isolation. When judging a price and considering the product's purchase, they compare it to other reference prices. Commonly used reference prices include competitors' prices, the company's historical prices, and other prices that the customer may encounter before purchase. Considering this pillar provides the range of prices customers find reasonable as a third data point for pricing decisions. Perceptive marketers can also influence which reference prices customers use and how they interpret them. We will examine the role of reference prices in Chapter 6.

The value proposition. As shown in Figure 2.1, every pricing decision must be grounded in the company's marketing strategy, and serve to advance and support its strategic objectives. The company's pricing must be consistent with the rest of its marketing activities. A value proposition is the formal expression of the firm's marketing strategy, describing the significance of the product's unique characteristics relative to competitors. By articulating what the company considers its most important points of differentiation, a value proposition provides guidelines and sets constraints for pricing activities. It determines how costs, customer value, and reference prices are weighted in the pricing decision. We will understand the role played by the company's value proposition in detail in Chapter 7.

To summarize, in the *value pricing framework*, costs set the floor (or the minimum limit) on prices. Customer value sets the ceiling (or the upper bound) on prices, and reference prices provide the range of reasonable prices as well as a means of influencing customer decisions. The product's price cannot be too far away from prices for comparable products, and from its previous prices. The fourth factor, the value proposition, determines the relative weights given to costs, customer value, and reference prices, in the pricing decision.

One core idea of this book is that instead of relying on just one or two factors in a casual or tradition-bound way, you must consider all four factors systematically when making pricing decisions. When the four pillars are considered carefully and used appropriately, it increases your chances of making informed pricing decisions and enjoying positive outcomes. Together, the four pillars provide the parameters within which to make pricing decisions. Once you understand the roles played by each factor, the pricing task will become a clearer, more manageable and repeatable process.

THE ROLE OF THE COMPANY'S VALUES

In addition to considering the four pillars systematically, good pricing decisions are harmonious with the company's values and business philosophy. Values articulate what the company believes in and what it stands for. They provide a broad guide for every strategic decision, including pricing decisions made by the company. Table 2.1 provides a list of broadly applicable and attractive company values. It describes each corporate value and provides examples of companies that have harmonized their pricing strategy with the value.

Company Value	Description and Influence on Pricing Strategy
Transparency	The company is open to customers about how it makes money, the process by which it sets prices, and its cost inputs. Where possible, it involves customers in the pricing process. Examples: Costco's famous restricted markup policy, online retailer Everlane's "radical transparency" approach of revealing its costs to customers.
Reliability	The company designs its price structure to create and communicate reliability and to engender trust. Example: The "ToyotaCare" no cost maintenance and service plan for the first two years of ownership of a Toyota car[11].
Flexibility	The company uses the latest data science and technology (e.g., dynamic pricing algorithms) to adjust prices frequently in response to demand and environmental factors. Example: The Houston Astros' dynamic pricing of single-game tickets in response to secondary

	market prices, Amazon's frequent price changes.
Excitement	The company generates excitement among customers by offering numerous, short-lived promotions and sales. Examples: Online retailer Woot's sequential promotions called Woot-offs, Kohl's frequent weekend, and special event sales.
Fairness	The company states its value proposition clearly and delivers on promises made to customers. Example: Disney's theme park ticket prices are relatively high and are raised periodically. In return, guests enjoy a memorable experience with constant augmentation that encourages repeat visits and a high degree of guest loyalty.
Value for Money	The company emphasizes low prices as the core of its value proposition and focuses on providing customers with high quality for low prices. Example: Discount supermarket Aldi keeps its operating costs low by encouraging self-service and sells products at prices significantly lower than the competition.
Superior Quality	The company emphasizes superior quality of customer experience through its pricing strategy. Example: Whole Foods Market positions itself as promoting consumer health and stocks nutritious foods, and assortments of natural and organic products at higher prices than competitors.
Luxury	The company builds an exclusive brand with high prestige and status value. It sells premium products at very high prices and margins. Example: Louis Vuitton sells its bags at high prices to create an aura of exclusivity. It never runs promotions and sells a small quantity of each design to create and maintain scarcity[12].

Table 2.1 Company values that influence pricing strategy

Even though company values are relatively abstract, they provide useful guidance to the manager for making business, and particularly, pricing, decisions. Take the example of transparency. When a company adopts transparency as a value, it pledges to make its external constituents such as customers, suppliers, investors, and the larger community in which it operates, privy to information that is usually held internally. Transparency is a particularly sensitive concern for the company's revenue and margin models. When a company is open and honest with customers about these models, the transparency creates a sense of trust and reciprocity. When it shares, not only its method but also actual figures, the transparency is even more palpable and appreciated. Transparency becomes the engine that drives the company's pricing strategy.

Consider the upscale startup online retailer Everlane. In the clothing industry, retailers are notoriously secretive about their costs, supply chains, and profit margins. In such an environment, Everlane has adopted the contrary value of "radical transparency" as its core philosophy. For every product it makes, it discloses its itemized costs on materials, labor, and transport, along with its markup percentage. As the advertising expert, Mike O'Toole pointed out, radical transparency is not just a pricing approach for the company[13]. It also guides the types of products the company chooses to sell. Instead of selling flimsy garments that wear out after a few washes, Everlane sells durable products. The company has adopted an unconventional approach to fashion, relying on sales of individual pieces instead of collections. According to O'Toole, "Transparency was a founding principle, not a me-too move... At Everlane, a singular idea has become a deep-seated cultural value—call it the soul of the company. And that is impossible to fake." Everlane is an excellent example of how company values influence every business decision it makes and how it harmonizes pricing strategy with its core values.

CHAPTER SUMMARY

In this chapter, we saw that pricing is the most effective lever available to managers and entrepreneurs to improve the company's profit. When prices are increased even by a small amount while maintaining sales and costs at existing levels, the company enjoys a significant boost in profit.

We considered how to define a good pricing decision. To do so, we distinguished between the decision's process and its outcome and argued that you should only be concerned with the process, leaving results to take care of themselves. We defined a good pricing decision as one that is made deliberately and thoughtfully. It considers the four pricing pillars—costs, customer value, reference prices and the value proposition, is based on the company's business philosophy and values, and can be explained to customers and to employees involved in implementing it.

We also introduced the roles of the four pillars of pricing. Costs set the floor, and customer value sets the ceiling, or the upper limit, on prices. The reference prices establish the range within which prices can be configured and will be considered as reasonable by customers, while the company's value proposition determines the relative weights given to costs, customer value, and reference prices in pricing decisions. Finally, the company's values, although abstract, deep-seated, and cultural in nature, exert a significant influence in guiding its pricing strategy. Good pricing decisions are harmonious with the company's values and business philosophy.

[3]

THE VALUE PRICING FRAMEWORK

So much the better. The higher the price you have to pay, the more you will cherish it. – Lloyd C. Douglas

In Chapter 2, we defined a good pricing decision as one that is made with deliberation, uses a structured process considering each of the four pricing pillars, and communicated unambiguously to customers and frontline employees responsible for implementing it. In this chapter, we will develop the structured process of making pricing decisions, called the *value pricing framework* in detail. In addition to the four pricing pillars as inputs, the framework distinguishes between two types of pricing decisions, setting new prices and changing existing prices, and acknowledges the importance of price execution. It also identifies four measures to evaluate pricing success, sales revenue, profit margin, customer satisfaction and employee satisfaction. And finally, it acknowledges the role played by the decision environment in affecting the process and outcomes of pricing decisions.

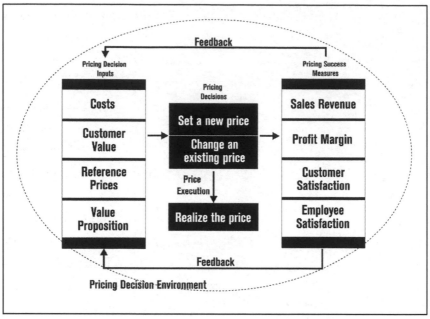

Figure 3.1 The value pricing framework

The *value pricing framework* is a flexible approach to making and evaluating pricing decisions that can be applied to any industry. The framework is just as suitable for a startup that is beginning to think about pricing, as it is for an established corporation with a complex portfolio of goods and services. Despite its flexibility, the *value pricing framework* is comprehensive and can inform managerial thinking about a variety of pricing issues.

The *value pricing framework* begins with the four primary inputs, the so-called four pillars of pricing. These include the company's costs that are relevant to the pricing decision, the customer's economic valuation of benefits provided by the product, the reference prices that customers already possess and those that are supplied by the company, and the value proposition that dictates how the three factors will be weighted in pricing. These four pricing decision inputs lead to two types of pricing decisions, setting a new price, and changing existing prices by increasing or decreasing them. Making these decisions also involves considering the pricing structure (whether to offer products a la carte, as bundles, or both, whether the prices have two parts, a fixed part and a variable part, up-front pricing vs. subscription, and so on). In practice, there is a significant gap between the quoted or listed prices in catalogs, store shelves, and websites, and what customers pay, after discounts, markdowns, freebies, and other incentives are factored in. Thus, we distinguish price realization, the actual prices paid by customers, from pricing decisions in the *value pricing framework* and consider why the gap between listed and realized prices occurs, and how to reduce it.

To determine the success of the organization's pricing decisions, the *value pricing framework* includes four measures: sales revenue, profit margin, customer satisfaction, and employee satisfaction. Instead of maximizing any one measure, an effective pricing strategy tries to balance the four measures. The key is to maintain or increase unit sales and revenue while enjoying a healthy profit margin, and having a base of customers that is satisfied with the company's prices and pricing policies, and proud, confident, and knowledgeable employees. This is the win-win-win-win quadfecta of the *value pricing framework*. However, when there are conflicts between the goals, as is often the case, the framework provides managers with the guidance on how to resolve them. The four pricing success measures, in turn, feed back to the pricing inputs, resulting in a cyclical process of price management that reflects the ongoing participation of customers and employees.

The final critical component of the framework is a consideration of the decision environment in which the company operates, and pricing decisions are made. A critical task of the manager is to monitor relevant economic, social, political, and technological factors and consider how these will affect the process described in the *value pricing framework*. The environment injects contingencies, opportunities, and increasingly, a greater dynamism that requires frequent price adjustments, and even a periodic consideration of the company's overall pricing strategy. In this chapter, we will understand the main ideas behind the *value pricing framework*, before exploring each major concept in the framework in detail in the chapters that follow.

THE PRICING DECISION INPUTS

We start our discussion of the *value pricing framework* with the four pricing decision inputs. As we have seen in Chapter 2, good pricing decisions rely on considering the four pillars of pricing carefully. Each pillar plays different roles individually, and together they guide the direction of a company's pricing strategy. Let us briefly consider the role of each decision input.

Costs are a necessary consideration in pricing decisions because, in the long run, the relationship between costs and prices is inescapable. For the company to be sustainable, its average prices must be greater than its average costs. Thus, costs establish the floor or lower bound of prices. Beyond this simple equation, however, understanding how costs change with the sales volume, and which costs to consider and which to ignore when making pricing decisions, are important considerations. Once the relevant costs are adequately understood, and a long-term viable pricing structure is put in place that is designed to cover average costs, managers have the flexibility to design creative short-term pricing offers to attract new customers or to increase sales to existing customers while adding to the company's profits.

Each of the product's many features potentially provides customer benefits. Customer value quantifies them by mapping the product's features to benefits, and benefits to the willingness to pay. For pricing decisions, customer value is significant because it is unrelated to its costs. Thus, it offers a unique data point about viable prices and helps to generate an upper bound on prices customers consider as worth paying. It also provides guidance on how to increase customer value in economically beneficial ways.

For example, customers often place tremendous significance on a feature that costs the company very little money to offer. When buying season ticket packages, sports fans are happy to pay a hefty premium for receiving priority for playoff tickets, a feature that costs a professional sports team virtually nothing to offer. On the other hand, customers may be willing to pay little or nothing for features that are very expensive to deliver. In early versions of Amazon's Kindle reading device, the text-to-speech feature was added at significant cost. However, few customers used this feature, leading Amazon to drop it in later versions to avoid dealing with objections from the publishing industry[1]. Knowing the "benefit to economic value translations" of customers allows the company to design and then make value-aligned pricing offers.

Customers rarely judge prices in absolute terms. When assessing whether a price is a "good price" or not, customers always evaluate it relative to other prices. These reference prices include prices that the customer is familiar with such as the product's old price, and the prices encountered during the purchase process such as those of key competitors, or even prices of unrelated products. Reference prices play dual roles of creating a frame of reference and helping the customer to form a range of prices that are deemed as reasonable for the product. Staying within this range of reasonable prices is an important consideration because customers tend to focus less on price and more on non-price attributes when prices are maintained within this range. The second role of reference prices is to persuade customers. By strategically supplying reference prices through cues such as using prices ending in 9, or a round number, or methods such as comparative advertising, the company can influence how customers judge the product's price[2].

The fourth pricing decision input is the company's value proposition, which articulates the product's core differentiators. Although it is the last of the four inputs in the *value pricing framework*, it is perhaps the most important and the most underappreciated input into pricing decisions. Without a strong value proposition, it is tough to have a strong pricing strategy. Moreover, on the flip side, as we will see in the Costco Wholesale case study later in this chapter, a differentiated and attractive value proposition wins half the pricing battle.

The value proposition concretizes the marketing strategy and values that the firm endorses, and provides a broad set of guidelines to make specific pricing decisions. Its primary function in the *value pricing framework* is to influence the relative weights managers give to the other three decision inputs. For example, a company that has built its brand and value proposition around a "value-for-money" positioning strategy, like the discount grocer Aldi, emphasizes its costs and its prices relative to competitors. It will price its products to remain significantly lower than its peers. In contrast, the fast-casual restaurant chain, Panera Bread, whose value proposition is "craveable wellness and elevated experiences," places greater emphasis on customer value and less on costs or reference prices. The upshot is that it will be willing to charge higher prices than its competitors, as long as they remain within the reasonable range of prices.

WHY SHOULD ALL FOUR DECISION INPUTS BE CONSIDERED?

Pricing decisions can easily be made by examining just one or at most two of the four pricing decision inputs. In fact, this is what most companies do. Take the example of pricing a restaurant menu. When setting menu prices, most restaurants estimate their costs and then mark them up by a certain predetermined percentage to arrive at the price.

While you may recognize this way of pricing a product as the cost-based pricing method, in the restaurant industry they even have a special name for it. It is called the Ideal Food Cost Pricing Model (IFC)[3]. When using the IFC model, restaurants first calculate their direct and indirect costs. Direct costs or food costs are the costs of ingredients that go into making the dishes. Indirect costs are non-food costs and include such expenses as the rent, utilities, labor costs, taxes, and insurance. Once these two costs have been calculated, then, somewhat arbitrarily, the operator sets an IFC percentage value. A common rule of thumb used in the industry is that IFC should be 30% of the menu price. A specific example will help you understand exactly how this works.

PRICING A MUSSELS APPETIZER IN A RESTAURANT

Let's say a plate of mussels cost the restaurant $3 to make. With the IFC method, it will be marked up to $3/30%, and listed at $10 on the menu. The logic behind this method is that the $7 markup will cover all the indirect food costs and generate a profit for the restaurant.

Additionally, some restaurants also consider the competitor's price as a second input. This approach is called the competition factor model because both food costs and competitors' prices are considered in setting menu prices. In pricing a plate of mussels, it may turn out that the restaurant's main competitor sells a comparable mussels appetizer for $12.50. Recall that the IFC method yielded a recommendation of $10. Using the competitor factor method provides a recommendation of $12.50. The restaurant will price the mussels dish somewhere between $10 and $12.50 using a combination of the two approaches.

According to the *value pricing framework*, using these two methods is an incomplete pricing decision, because only some of the relevant information is utilized. The operator did not consider the restaurant's value proposition, that is, the image it wants to convey to guests with its menu prices. Is it a neighborhood café that customers visit for dinner several times a week? Alternatively, is it a special event destination restaurant where couples go for a celebration dinner or to get engaged? It makes little sense to charge the same price for the mussels appetizer in these two cases. In fact, irrespective of costs or competitor prices, we would expect the dish to have a significantly higher price in the destination restaurant than in the neighborhood café[4].

Nor did the restaurant consider how much its customers value a plate of mussels (let's say it is no more than $15), or whether the item can be offered for a higher price during a certain period of the year. For instance, it could be that the restaurant has received positive reviews from famous food critics and bloggers, and patrons are clamoring for a reservation. Or the city is in the middle of a deep recession, and hardly anyone wants to spend $10, let alone $12, for an appetizer. Or mussels are a hot food trend this year, and everyone wants to eat mussels. Each of these situations will warrant a different price.

The restaurant would consider its value proposition, customer value, and the pricing environment in addition to its costs and reference prices to determine a price for its mussels appetizer (and everything else on its menu) when using the *value pricing framework*.

Figure 3.2 summarizes the role played by the four decision inputs in pricing the appetizer. Costs set the floor, meaning that the restaurant must charge more than $3 for it. Since customers are unwilling to pay more than $15, this is the ceiling on price. The prices of the two major competitors, $10 and $12.50, and the restaurant's own previous price, $9.50, provide the reference prices, forming the range of reasonable prices. The restaurant's value proposition, to serve as a neighborhood café, dictates the weights that will be assigned to costs (W1), customer value (W2), and reference prices (W3). Because it wants to be seen as an affordable restaurant to visit frequently for dinner, it may choose

to keep prices close to its competitors' prices, weighting reference prices more, and costs and customer value to a lesser degree.

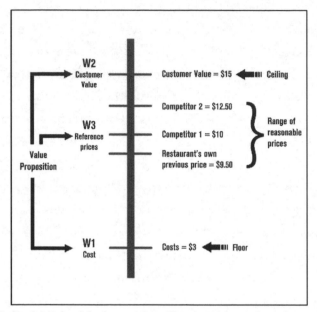

Figure 3.2 Role of the four pricing pillars in pricing a plate of mussels

PRICING THE NEXT-GEN PRIUS IN 2015

As we said earlier, pricing decisions never happen in a vacuum. The context, or what we can call the *pricing decision environment* in the *value pricing framework*, is an important
consideration. The pricing of the Toyota Prius hybrid car illustrates the importance of the decision environment. Ever since it
was launched in the late 1990s, the Prius has remained a best
seller for Toyota, garnering rave reviews and leading the hybrid
sedan category in sales year after year. In its latest generation
introduced in 2015, Prius' already stellar fuel economy increased
further to a whopping 54 miles per gallon. Toyota designers also

upgraded its styling by adding a sleek new look. It was clear to industry experts that this next generation of the Toyota Prius delivered a lot more value to buyers when compared to the previous generation.

If we were to analyze Prius' pricing power and sales prospects using costs, customer value, reference prices, and the value proposition, all four inputs would suggest that Toyota could easily raise the 2016 Prius' price. The costs to manufacture a Prius remained more or less unchanged. However, when compared to reference points such as prices of other hybrids and the previous generation Prius, the new version offered significantly greater value to customers.

In Prius' case, however, the pricing environment played a decisive role in invalidating this logic. Even as Toyota maintained its prices for the superior 2016 Prius, its sales never took off. In fact, unit sales of the automobile plummeted by 26% year-over-year during the first half of 2016. The main culprit was the economic environment, in particular, low gasoline prices. In explaining poor sales, Toyota dealer Brendan Harrington told the Wall Street Journal, "That's not because of the car. The entire market has dramatically shifted to light trucks and SUVs with gas under $3 a gallon[5]."

The moral of this case study is that the company can have a terrific product that offers superior value to the customer. Still, whether it is able to charge a higher price will depend on the environment's cooperation. In a high gas price environment, the 2016 Prii would have literally driven themselves off dealers' lots even with a hefty price hike. However, because the gas prices were so low, Toyota could not even maintain its Prius sales with prices that offered superior value to customers.

Customer value and other pricing decision inputs are not fixed quantities that are waiting to be measured, combined, and converted into a corresponding price. For Toyota Prius, the value derived by customers was a moving target. It was contingent on the environment in which the customers and the company operated. The same thing is true of the other pricing decision inputs. Each input is affected by the environment. Effective pricing decisions can only be made after understanding and accounting for how the pricing environment affects the four decision inputs.

SETTING NEW PRICES AND CHANGING EXISTING PRICES

In the value pricing framework, managers overwhelmingly make two types of pricing decisions: they either set a new price or they change an existing price. Pricing expert Fred Emery made a further distinction by suggesting that setting new prices and changing existing prices can each fall into two categories. This distinction leads to four types of pricing decisions that vary in difficulty and the weights given to the decision inputs. Although it was made in the 1960s, even today, Emery's distinction is helpful to managers in untangling the nuances of different pricing decisions:

- **Pricing an entirely new product.** When pricing a radical innovation, the company has no precedent. Its task is challenging. It relies on understanding and utilizing each of the four decision inputs by starting with a blank slate and paying particular attention to customer value and the company's value proposition. The significance of this pricing decision also lies in the fact that it will dictate future prices and competitor responses.

- **Pricing a new version of an existing product.** To align with today's rapid pace of innovation, companies must set prices for improved versions or next generations of products and services, whether it is breakfast cereal, a patio chair, a smartphone, or a new thresher for commercial farms. For such decisions, the previous version or generation's price plays an important role. It serves as an established precedent that customers will use to evaluate the product's improvements, and decide whether the price increment is worth paying for.

- **Changing the price in response to changing business characteristics.** The impetus for this pricing decision arises from changing cost levels or cost structures due to modified formulation, changes in product ingredients or the replacement of high-cost channels with lower cost ones. Such price changes also arise from changes in management's goals, such as when a new CEO comes in and proclaims that she wants 20% sales growth next year, or from changes to the line-up of the organization's suppliers or channel members. Finally, prices are modified when competitors change prices. For this pricing decision, the customer's value equation remains unchanged. Thus, prices change to the extent that costs and reference prices are weighted more heavily by the company in its decision calculus.

- **Changing the price to meet changing customer preferences.** The last type of pricing decision is driven by changes in customer perceptions of value derived from the product. Value perceptions change when consumer expectations change, such as when new alternatives become available in the market, or the economic environment shifts and leads to significant changes in customer behavior. The manager focuses primarily on understanding how customer value has changed.

Most pricing decisions are price changes. Managers do not get the opportunity to set first-time prices for radical innovations or even for new versions of existing products very often. Such decisions only occur when a product is introduced to a market. In most companies, 90% or even more of pricing decisions involve changing prices from current levels, adjusting them in response to shifts in one of the four decision inputs, or due to a change in the pricing environment. Just as important is the fact that most price changes are small in magnitude and percentage terms. It is rare and risky to increase list prices by double-digit percentages. Likewise, it is unusual to lower list prices dramatically, except for specific, idiosyncratic purposes such as to get rid of old inventory or damaged products.

Another important distinction in the *value pricing framework* is between strategic and tactical pricing decisions. In April 2014, the Indianapolis Zoo changed its pricing structure from a fixed ticket price to variable pricing in which all future ticket prices change every day based on the number of tickets already sold and forecasted demand. Visitors to the zoo who purchase their tickets in advance are rewarded, and those who wait until the last minute pay the highest price. Similarly, the Houston Astros Major League Baseball team shifted from a fixed price strategy to a dynamic pricing approach in 2012, dramatically increasing how often they changed single-game ticket prices[6]. These are examples of strategic pricing decisions.

In contrast, department stores like J. C. Penney and Kohl's often run one-day or weekend sales when prices for certain product categories are discounted for a limited time. My neighborhood Sprouts Farmers Market grocery store has different items on promotional pricing each week on a rotating or seasonal basis. These are examples of tactical price changes where choosing which categories or brands to promote and the level of discount to offer are the primary targets of the pricing decision. A vast majority of pricing decisions are of this latter type. They are day-to-day tactical price changes of small magnitude.

PRICE EXECUTION

The *value pricing framework* also distinguishes between pricing decisions and price execution. This is because, as we saw earlier, there is a gap between prices companies ask for and what they get. It is one thing to quote a price, another entirely to receive payment for the full amount. In business markets, customers may get a quantity discount, an allowance to run an advertising campaign, free freight, or an additional discount for prompt payment. In consumer markets, customers may use a coupon, buy during an exclusive flash sale, receive a promotional giveaway, or pay less because they belong to a rewards program. These are just some examples of incentives received by customers. Each incentive adds to the gap between the asked-for price and the earned price.

For a company, the price realization gap can be significant and undermine its pricing effectiveness. When the 2017 Toyota

Prius was launched, its listed base price was $30,960. But this price meant little to customers. They only paid an average of $28,352, a gap of 8.4%. Even worse, a fifth of Prius owners paid less than $27,513, resulting in a price realization gap of 11%[7]. In business markets, a cement manufacturer listed one of its products at $11.97 in its price lists. When all incentives given to customers were taken into account, however, it was only earning $6.53 per bag sold. Put differently, its price realization gap was 45.4%[8].

To understand the extent of harm created by this gap, consider a mountaineer who decides to climb Mount Everest and spends two years to prepare and plan for this herculean task. When the time comes to climb the mountain, he only ends up reaching the first base camp before turning back. The mountaineer's decision-making process was admirable, but his execution was lacking. The price that a company decides to charge is like Mount Everest, the process by which it is determined is analogous to the mountaineer's planning, and price execution is how high he is actually able to climb on his expedition. Notice that in this analogy, the reason why the mountaineer turned back may have to do with his physical fitness, his support team, or external factors such as bad weather. The same is true of price realization. Both the company and the environment affect price execution. Making a good pricing decision is only meaningful when it is implemented, and the asked-for price is earned by the company. Otherwise, it is just like a mountaineer charting an elaborate plan to climb Mount Everest, but only getting to its foothills.

Why does the price realization gap occur? There are many reasons, and their consideration will be the focus of Chapter 8.

One factor has to do with simply not knowing what the gap is, and how many and what amounts of incentives customers are receiving. A second reason concerns which managers within the company, if any, have responsibility for price execution, and how they are compensated for managing the gap. Third, price execution may fall outside the domain or responsibility of managers who make pricing decisions, and the company's pricing philosophy and guidelines for price execution are simply not communicated properly to frontline employees. These managers may carefully go through a process in which they consider the decision inputs carefully before setting prices. However, someone entirely different within the company, say salespeople, then take over the negotiation process. How the negotiation unfolds and what concessions are given will dictate the size of the price realization gap.

A significant amount of recent academic research has begun to understand how to close the price realization gap, and we shall examine some of it in Chapter 8. The main point to make here is that, for the firm's pricing strategy to be successful, price execution is just as important as making good pricing decisions. Doing all the work to figure out the best price to charge customers loses its shine if the customers only pay a fraction of the price.

MEASURING PRICING SUCCESS

The last part of the *value pricing framework* measures the success of pricing decisions and price execution. Intuitively but incorrectly, many managers think of effective pricing in terms of sales maximization or profit margin maximization goals. While both sales and profits are obviously important, it rarely makes sense to charge prices that will attract the most number of customers or sell the most number of units, or even generate the highest amount of revenue. The company could simply price its products low to achieve such goals. Nor are companies advised to earn the maximum profit margin. To do so, it could set the price in the highest possible range, close to the price ceiling, sell a few units of the product, and earn a high profit margin.

The fact is that these two goals of financial performance, increasing sales and increasing profit margin, conflict with each other. One goal can be achieved only at the other's expense. Companies can "buy" unit sales by sacrificing profit margin, or they can be selective, giving up sales and increasing margin. Complicating things even further, pricing not only affects the company's financial performance as measured by its sales and profits, but it also has significant effects on customer and employee satisfaction.

Customers love to buy from companies whose pricing strategies reflect their own values and whose prices are fair, transparent, stable and aligned with the economic value delivered by products. Just witness how consumers still flock to stores every time a new Nintendo gaming console or Apple iPhone is released. These items are not cheap, but customers find their prices to be congenial. On the other hand, consider online retailers who are constantly changing prices of products, up to several times a day. As we will discuss in Chapter 9, customers hate this volatility in prices because it complicates their buying decision and makes it hard to form or use reference prices. Such pricing dissatisfies customers. Along similar lines, there is a trade-off between financial performance and customer satisfaction. Giving customers more and more benefits will increase their satisfaction, but without commensurate price increases, this will be a recipe for profit erosion.

For employees, a well-strategized and well-executed pricing strategy is a source of organizational pride. When prices are explained, align with common sense, and come across as fair, they are easy to communicate to customers, and defend when making sales. Such pricing contributes to creating an aura of competence around the company that provides confidence to employees and boosts their morale. On the other hand, when a company adopts an "aggressive growth at any price" mentality and embarks on the path of offering discounts willy-nilly, employees lose their confidence in the products they are selling and become confused and embarrassed.

These soft, people-based measures are often overlooked and ignored by managers, even though customer and employee reactions to pricing decisions are what lead to success or failure. With the *value pricing framework*, the manager tries to balance the four success measures. They not only pay attention to changes in financial measures of pricing performance, they are also sensitive to the reactions of customers and employees to the company's pricing decisions and price execution.

The *pricing audit* provided in the Appendix at the end of this book is a structured questionnaire that takes you through each component of the *value pricing framework* and helps you gauge how well your organization is applying its principles when making pricing decisions. Next, let us consider a detailed case study of the *value pricing framework* in practice.

COSTCO WHOLESALE: THE POSTER CHILD FOR THE VALUE PRICING FRAMEWORK

Even as its competitors struggle to survive, Costco Wholesale remains "Amazon proof." Its pricing strategy is an important reason for its remarkable success[9]. Costco is the largest warehouse chain in the world, with more than 720 locations and $116 billion in annual revenue as of 2016[10]. It has carved out a large retailing niche for itself, attracting a base of loyal customers who love shopping for the differentiated and high-quality products that are found at attractive prices in its stores. Approximately 3 million customers shop at a Costco store on any given day. Costco's business model and pricing strategy contravene many rules of traditional retailing strategy, but it is a poster child for this book's *value pricing framework.*

UNCONVENTIONAL, DIFFERENTIATED VALUE PROPOSITION

Costco's value proposition to its shoppers is "no-frills" physical shopping of differentiated, high-quality products in bulk for low prices. While Walmart's low price positioning has been well documented and admired by business experts for decades, one can argue that Costco's value-price positioning is even more potent. From store design to product display, from assortment to prices, every single aspect of the company's offering communicates value to its customers. Each Costco Wholesale store aims to appear like a warehouse. The company's co-founder said in a television interview, "We try to create an image of a warehouse type of an environment. I once joked it costs a lot of money to make these places look cheap. But we spend a lot of time and energy in trying to create that image. This is a value place. But you need to deliver[11]."

The company takes great trouble to infuse authenticity into its "no-frills" image because it is such a core part of its value proposition. A Costco store's floors are bare concrete slabs. They are cheaper to install, are more durable, and require less maintenance than linoleum or carpet. Its ceilings are steel beams and have huge skylights to reduce electricity consumption. Merchandise is rolled out and displayed in the store on the same industrial pallets on which it is brought in by trucks, reducing the cost of unpacking and setting up displays.

In a Costco warehouse, the available assortment is meager, especially when compared to competitors. A typical store only stocks about 4,000 different items at any given time. In comparison, a Target store carries around 80,000 items[12] and a neighborhood supermarket has close to 40,000 items[13]. Costco Wholesale pays its employees much higher wages than the industry average. Its employees earn an average of $20 an hour, and more than 90 percent receive benefits, including health insurance. Not surprisingly, employee satisfaction rates are the highest, and employee turnover rates are among the lowest in the retail industry. In its entirety, Costco's value proposition, which is firmly rooted in a clearly-articulated set of values, is virtually impossible to replicate.

WELL-PUBLICIZED AND HONESTLY APPLIED SMALL MERCHANDISE MARKUP

Costco's pricing strategy is simple[14]. It buys merchandise in bulk from manufacturers, obtaining it at much lower costs than its peers. In direct opposition to the conventional wisdom, Costco widely and regularly publicizes its use of a cost-plus approach to pricing. In fact, markup pricing is a core component of the Costco brand and one of the first things customers know about it. Although it does not provide details about how much each product has been marked up, its average markup is 12 percent. The company also mandates nothing in the store can be marked up by more than 14 percent (except for its private label products, where they can be marked up one whole percentage point higher at 15%). Most supermarkets and department stores also use markup pricing. However, their average markups are 25 percent for a supermarket, and 100 percent for a department store. Also, their markups vary drastically by product. It is common for some products in a supermarket such as the olive bar, bakery items, and brand name spices to be marked up by several hundred percent[15].

To appreciate how radical Costco's markup pricing approach is, consider the following example provided by Nina Shapiro in 2006[16]. In the late 1990s, Costco started selling all-cotton, button-down shirts in its stores for $17.99. When it first introduced the product, it committed to buying at least 100,000 pieces of the shirt from the manufacturer. Over the years, the shirts were so popular at the $17.99 price that by 2006, the company was selling over a million pieces. Because of this high volume, it was able to negotiate an even lower price. It could have pocketed the resultant cost savings. However, Costco was so wedded to its mandated markup policy, it promptly passed on the cost savings to customers, lowering the already low prices of the shirt to $12.99. When asked whether it was tempted to maintain prices, Costco's then-CEO Jim Sinegal remarked, "Who the hell's going to notice if you charge $14.99 [instead of 12.99]? Well, we're going to know. It's an attitudinal thing—you always give the customer the best deal." This is the essence of the *value pricing framework* in practice; the company gives greater weight to customer value because of its value proposition, and balances customers' satisfaction against its desire to make the highest revenue or profit.

The prices of items sold in Costco's food court provide another compelling example of its consistent pricing approach. Calling these offerings "recession-proof and inflation-proof," the company has maintained the same prices for decades. For instance, the iconic "hot dog and soda" combo has remained at $1.50 since 1985 when it was first offered, while the size of the soda increased from a 12 oz. can to a 20 oz. fountain drink. Similarly, the 18-inch pizza's price and quality has remained unchanged since 1989. It was sold at $9.95 then, as it is today. It is not surprising that a ritualistic part of many customers' shopping trips is to visit Costco's food court and have a meal there. How does Costco do it? According to an assessment in its Costco Connections customer magazine, "it's a very controlled business model aimed at streamlined service. It's much like the warehouse: the most popular and the best-quality items instead of a wide range of prices[17]. " Again, we see consistency in the value proposition and the central role that pricing decisions play in its delivery.

ANNUAL MEMBERSHIP FEE

Costco Wholesale uses a classic two-dimensional pricing strategy, the economics of which are opaque to many shoppers. To supplement the low markups of merchandise and to boost its profits, Costco charges an annual membership price to customers. Its membership price is currently $55 for individuals and $115 for small businesses. Only those who are Costco members have access to its stores and services; you cannot just walk off the street and shop in a Costco store. What is more, close to 90 percent of its 44.6 million members renew their memberships each year, providing it with a large stable revenue stream, $2.6 billion in 2015[18].

This two-dimensional pricing approach has a dramatic positive impact on customers' perceptions of Costco's pricing. Costco customers pay the annual fee once each year and then promptly forget about it. This "price of entry" recedes to the background for most shoppers and does not factor in their calculations of the actual prices paid for products purchased at Costco. The only value the customer receives for the membership fee is access to Costco's stores for a year. The merchandise prices encountered on every shopping trip are far more visible to shoppers. These frequently encountered prices are significantly lower than competitors, and create and sustain the favorable low-price image in consumers' minds. What is more, memberships also impose switching costs on customers, making Costco a more attractive place to shop regularly. This gives a distinctive competitive advantage to the retailer.

ORIGINAL PRICE LABEL VOCABULARY

Engaging and satisfying customers and employees with prices involves more than just offering them superior value. In addition to its already low shelf prices, Costco Wholesale employs a transparent and extensive vocabulary on its price labels to further communicate the degree of value in its stores[19]. Specific prices and symbols placed on price labels have specific meanings that provide useful cues. This vocabulary is well known to Costco enthusiasts and is part of the customer's socialization process. Knowledge of this is seen as a status symbol, expressing love for the Costco brand and frugality as a value of those who shop there[20]. For example, a price that ends in .97 at Costco means that the product has been marked down even further from its original marked price, and represents a real bargain. A price that has an asterisk on the label indicates that the product is a close-out and will not return, similar to a "last call" in a bar. Prices that end in .88 or .00 are manager markdowns of merchandise that have some blemishes (such as a damaged box) but are perfectly serviceable. Customers enjoy interpreting these prices and employees enjoy teaching customers this vocabulary.

LESSONS FROM COSTCO WHOLESALE'S PRICING STRATEGY

Costco Wholesale uses virtually every one of the principles outlined in the *value pricing framework* with finesse and outstanding results. Considering the pricing decision inputs first, it has an excellent handle on costs and makes quick work of competitors' prices. Its two-dimensional pricing strategy was pioneering in this industry, generating a competitive pricing advantage for Costco. It can sell products in its stores at close to breakeven. The markup of 12% on store sales helps cover its fixed costs. Coupled with low prices negotiated with suppliers due to high volume purchases and willingness to accept products in irregular cycles, shoppers enjoy significantly lower prices at Costco relative to its competitors. The second dimension, the annual membership fees paid by each Costco member, generates revenues that flow straight to Costco's bottom line. The company has portrayed a low-price image through its low actual prices and a warehouse ambiance, which produces a compelling value proposition for its huge target customer base. Considering its pricing actions, Costco uses price changes to create a unique vocabulary that enhances its relationship with loyal shoppers. Not surprisingly, its revenues have grown strongly, it has been able to maintain a healthy profit margin in the extremely competitive retailing industry, and it has the most satisfied customers and employees anywhere. With its unique perspective on why it is in business and how to conduct its activities, and by using its pricing strategy to advance both these perspectives, Costco is a poster child for the *value pricing framework*.

CHAPTER SUMMARY

In this chapter, we considered the steps involved in making pricing decisions with a structured, methodical approach called the *value pricing framework*. We saw that the framework considers the four pillars of pricing introduced in Chapter 2 as the four key inputs into making pricing decisions. The manager gives appropriate weights to the company's relevant costs, customer value, and reference prices, depending on the product's value proposition. With this procedure, every pricing decision is grounded in, and influenced by, the company's marketing strategy.

The *value pricing framework* distinguishes between two main types of pricing decisions, setting a new price, and changing existing prices by increasing or decreasing them. When considering price changes, both magnitude and frequency of the change are important considerations. Because most companies have a significant gap between listed or quoted prices and the prices customers pay, we recognized the importance of price execution and of minimizing the price realization gap.

We also saw that rather than considering financial measures of pricing success such as sales revenue and profit margin alone, the *value pricing framework* also pays attention to the softer people-based measures of customer and employee reactions to the company's pricing strategy. Rather than emphasizing just one measure, effective pricing decisions are those that try to balance all four measures. A good pricing strategy strives to maintain or increase sales revenue while producing a healthy profit margin, a base of customers that are satisfied with the company's prices and pricing policies, and proud, confident, and knowledgeable employees. Finally, we studied the case of Costco Wholesale as a poster child for the principles of the *value pricing framework*.

[4]

Costs

You'd be surprised how expensive it costs to look this cheap. –
Steven Tyler

In the *value pricing framework*, costs are a necessary input
into every pricing decision. Without knowing the product's
costs accurately or using them appropriately, the framework's objectives of making effective pricing decisions, minimizing the price realization gap, and achieving a balance between
the conflicting outcomes of sales revenue, profit margin, customer satisfaction, and employee satisfaction cannot be reached.

Companies routinely make the mistake of setting prices based
solely on costs. Consider the decision of movie studios on how
much to charge for electronic rentals of new movies within days
of their release in movie theaters. When movie studios like
Warner Bros. and Fox made this decision recently, they focused
only on costs (factoring in the amount they would have to share
with movie theaters to appease them). With a cost-based method,
they settled on prices between $25 and $50 for each rental. With

the abundant choice of slightly older movies available on demand for \$4–\$6 from Amazon, iTunes, and Google Play, not to mention the streaming content from Netflix, these prices appeared ludicrously high to most consumers, and they rejected the new service resoundingly[1]. A far lower price would still have been profitable, but it was never considered because it did not cover costs.

In a nutshell, here's how to think about costs when making pricing decisions: *Effective prices are rarely set or changed based solely on costs. However, without considering costs, prices would be like anchorless ships adrift on the ocean, just as likely to reach a port, as they are to float away and disappear over the horizon.* Simply put, understanding costs and how they change with the price is essential to making good pricing decisions. We will develop this idea in detail throughout this chapter.

COSTS AND PRICES: THE CHICKEN OR THE EGG?

Which one comes first, costs or prices? This question is almost as tricky and difficult to answer as the classic chicken or egg causality dilemma. Consider Gillette, the brand behind such premium quality razors as the Fusion and Mach series. In the United States, once consumers have purchased one of Gillette's razors, each replacement blade cartridge costs several dollars. With more than 80% of the US razor market share, these products are extremely profitable for Gillette, and its parent company, P&G[2].

When Gillette wanted to enter the Indian market in 2007, however, these prices were simply beyond the grasp of all but the richest strata of Indian consumers. P&G responded by conducting extensive marketing research with thousands of Indian men, understanding how they shaved, and how much money they could afford to spend. With this knowledge, the company designed a razor system that was much simpler than the Fusion or the Mach. This product, unique to India, was called the Gillette Guard and was priced at 30 cents for the razor, and 10 cents for each cartridge. It was tremendously successful, taking over 60 percent of the Indian razor market within two years[3]. For Gillette Guard, the product's price came first, and its costs were engineered afterward by the company.

In the *value pricing framework*, however, we will give precedence to costs, viewing them as a crucial input into the company's pricing decisions (see Figure 3.1). In our discussion, costs come first prices come later. This is because companies rarely have the opportunity, as P&G did in India, to conduct a clean-slate needs assessment of customers, and develop an entirely new product from the ground up with a target price to aim for. In the rare instance that you get such an opportunity, you should grab it with both hands! However, in the hundreds of pricing decisions I have witnessed, not even a handful have been of this type. Bread-and-butter pricing decisions are made after the company has an established infrastructure, supply chain, production, distribution, and communication processes, for which many costs have already been incurred, and others are ongoing or forthcoming. In this book, our mantra is *costs come first, and then come prices.*

THE DUAL ROLES OF COSTS IN THE VALUE PRICING FRAMEWORK

When making pricing decisions, costs should always be considered, but in tandem with the other decision inputs. Understanding the product's costs and how they vary with changes in the product's quality and quantity is critical to the company's pricing success.

In this chapter, we will study two different roles played by costs in pricing decisions. Their first task is to establish the lower bound of prices. This role is tricky, however, because there are two different lower bounds or floors to be considered. We will discuss the concepts of *incremental costs* and *irrelevant costs* to understand which costs are relevant, and which ones should be ignored when making pricing decisions. We will also describe the idea of a *price floor* and distinguish between two types of price floors; *long-term price floors* that account for all product costs, and *short-term price floors*, that only cover incremental costs. Long-term price floors ensure the company's financial viability. Short-term price floors provide managers with the flexibility to devise creative short-term pricing methods and develop offers that, if used judiciously, can lead to positive outcomes. We will study how Broadway theaters, travel discounter Priceline, and Heinz Ketchup all use short-term price floors to bolster their respective bottom lines. When conceiving of costs as supplying a floor for prices, the most common application is to choose a markup percentage and calculate the price based on costs alone. We will understand the logic behind this *cost-based pricing method*, learn the difference between *markup pricing* and *cost-plus pricing*, and the weaknesses associated with the cost-based pricing method.

The second important role of costs is to serve as the centerpiece of the firm's marketing strategy. When the company has a cost advantage over its competitors, or when it can use its cost structure to craft a strong value proposition, and deliver it consistently to customers, costs become an integral part of the brand identity, and can exert a strong influence on consumer behaviors. Just consider the brand strength of warehouse discounter Costco that we saw earlier, or the business model of startup clothing retailer Everlane that is founded on the core value of "radical transparency." Both companies have credited their hawk-like attention to costs and their strategic utilization of costs for their success. Many other companies such as Aldi, Walmart, and Taco Bell[4] use cost leadership successfully as a business strategy. We will understand why cost leadership is such an efficient pricing and marketing strategy, and discuss what you can learn from it for potential application in your organization.

INCREMENTAL COSTS AND IRRELEVANT COSTS

When deciding to enter a market, sell a new product, or change prices, the manager must consider every future cost. Several years ago, I worked with a startup that was thinking of licensing GPS tracking technology and developing a new product that would allow a fleet of vehicles to be monitored in real time from a central location. Ambulance services, tow-truck operators, taxicab, and commercial trucking companies were all potential customers for this product. While such a concept may seem obsolete today with the widespread use of app-based tracking services through smartphones, at the time, it was a real innovation with much promise.

When the startup added all the costs it would incur to develop, manufacture, and launch the new product—which included software licensing fees, the costs of development, manufacturing and inventorying the hardware, sales and marketing costs, and costs of training and customer service—it became clear that the total cost of bringing the product to market was far too high. No reasonable price would cover all these costs. The firm decided not to move forward with this product and went on to explore other growth opportunities.

In this example, the startup was investigating the potential for a new product launch. With such launch decisions, considering every single future cost is important. This is because none of the money has been spent yet. In contrast, imagine a company that already has developed, designed, and manufactured the product and now wants to price it. Should the development, design, and manufacturing expenses that have already been incurred still be considered in the pricing decision? The short answer is no.

When considering costs as a decision input in the *value pricing framework*, we must make the fundamental distinction between costs that matter for pricing decisions and those that do not. Some costs are relevant to the pricing decision and must be considered, while others have no impact and must be ignored. When building pricing models, analysts refer to relevant costs as "incremental costs" and the costs to be ignored as "irrelevant costs.[5]"

The categories of incremental costs and irrelevant costs overlap with, but are not identical to, the well-known distinction between variable costs and fixed costs. *Variable costs* are those that change with the level of activity, say the quantity of product manufactured in a factory, or the number of sales made in a store. The cost of the rubber that goes into making a car tire, the transaction fees that Walmart pays Visa each time a shopper uses a Visa credit card in one of its stores, the commission paid by a seller to eBay when a listed item gets sold, the performance royalty paid by Spotify or a radio station to Justin Bieber each time they play "Love Yourself,[6]" and the per-hour fees that a strategy consultant bills her client are all examples of variable costs. Each of these costs changes with the activity level.

Other costs remain the same regardless of activity level. The tire company has to pay for its building and machinery each month regardless of the number of tires manufactured. Walmart has to pay its store manager's salary no matter how many shoppers visit the store, and an eBay seller has to pay the monthly rent of the locker where she stores her merchandise whether she makes any sales or not. These costs are called *fixed costs*. In a 1960 article, management professor Tom Kempner made the further distinction between "once-for-all" fixed costs and recurring fixed costs, which is helpful to our discussion[7]. All the examples just covered are those of recurring fixed costs that tend to be associated with a particular period instead of activity level. Typical recurring fixed costs include rent or lease on a building or factory, salaries of full-time employees, insurance, and advertising expenses.

Once-for-all fixed costs may be such things as the legal fees to set up a business, the costs of designing a new brand logo, slogans, and other elements for a startup, and so on. For pricing decisions, some recurring fixed costs may be incremental to the pricing decision if they are affected by the change in sales volume, while others may be irrelevant. Entrepreneurs take note; once-for-all fixed costs are always irrelevant to the pricing decision. However, as we saw with the case of the GPS tracking technology company, they can influence whether you want to go ahead with your project in the first place.

Many costs tend to be neither fully fixed nor entirely variable. These costs are referred to as *semi-variable costs*. Some parts of semi-variable costs are fixed, and others are variable. To give one example, many utilities charge a per-month service fee to commercial customers, which is the fixed component of the cost. The price of each kilowatt-hour of electricity used is the variable cost. Similarly, for a Costco customer, the annual membership fee is a fixed cost, and the cost of purchases is the variable cost.

PRICING A STEAKHOUSE SPECIAL

Now that we have covered different types of costs, let's understand how to distinguish between incremental and irrelevant costs with some examples. Imagine that a steakhouse puts a popular steak dish from its menu on special, offering it at a 20% reduced price for a day. Because of this promotion, the sales of the steak will increase. With each steak that is sold, the restaurant will incur variable costs of the meat and other ingredients on the plate. The restaurant's gross margin on the steak = Steak price - Variable costs. However, none of its fixed costs such as its rent, the chef's salary, the kitchen equipment leasing costs, or the electricity bill, will change if the steak is put on special.

Consequently, the restaurant should only consider its variable costs in deciding whether to offer the steak special. These are the only costs that are incremental to the decision of whether to provide the steak special or not. The fixed costs are irrelevant because they will be incurred anyway. The steakhouse manager must consider one other cost in this pricing decision. Economists refer to it as the opportunity cost, which is the cost of not selling other menu items at a potentially higher, full price, and earning a higher profit margin because the customer ordered the steak special instead. For example, if the steak special cannibalizes too many profitable roast chicken sales, the promotion may not be such a good idea and will have to be called off.

PRICING A SET MENU

To illustrate the subtlety associated with classifying costs as either incremental or irrelevant, let's consider another example, again from the restaurant industry. Imagine you run a restaurant. Business is good, but you could use a few more customers, especially for dinner during weekdays. So you decide to offer and promote a three-course set menu for $22. Which costs should you consider in making this decision?

First, regardless of whether you offer the set menu or not your fixed costs will be unaffected, just like the steakhouse in the previous example. So all fixed costs are irrelevant to the pricing decision. This is not the case, however, for variable costs. For every new customer that comes in because of the $22 set menu, the business will incur variable costs such as the costs of ingredients, credit card fees, clean linen, and carryout boxes for leftovers. These costs all have to be factored into your pricing decision.

There are still other subtle costs to consider here. You may have to print new menus or wish to promote the set menu offer on your website or app. Dealing with these costs is a bit trickier for the pricing decision. If you print new menus every day and will not incur any additional costs because of the set menu offer, the costs of printing the usual number of menus are not variable to the pricing decision and are irrelevant. (We will ignore the cost of extra ink to print the offer). However, if you have to print more menus than usual because the set menu increases customer count, you will have to include the cost of this fraction of excess menus as an incremental cost in your pricing decision. Also, if you have to print entirely new menus just for the set menu offer, or print and laminate table signs to advertise the set menu, then the costs of the new menus or table signs are incremental and must be included.

Calculating the restaurant's opportunity costs is also a bit harder than the previous example. If the customer would have ordered the three courses without the set menu offer, no opportunity cost is incurred. If they had ordered something instead, then there is the opportunity cost of not selling that item or items that should be considered.

There is one last important point to note. The set menu offer does not have to be at a discounted price to count as a pricing decision and trigger cost considerations. Even if you simply print new menus and offer a set menu bundle at a price that is the sum of the individual course prices (Set menu price = $22; Individual prices: Appetizer = $6, Entrée = $11, and dessert = $5), all of the prior discussion about incremental and irrelevant costs is just as applicable. Even though actual prices have not changed, the customer's perception of value derived from the set menu bundle has changed. This will influence purchases of menu items (by bringing in new business, and getting existing patrons to order that extra item because of the set menu).

This example illustrates an important lesson of the *value pricing framework*. Pricing decisions do not always have to be about raising or lowering prices from their current levels. They can also be about making price offers in different, creative ways, where the customer perceives that the value provided by the company has increased significantly, even when actual prices have not changed or gone up.

SHOULD YOU BECOME AN UBER/ LYFT DRIVER?

Pricing concepts can often help us answer real-life questions that, at first glance, do not seem to have anything to do with pricing. Let's apply the concepts of incremental and irrelevant costs to the decision of whether to become an Uber or Lyft driver. To make a good decision about taking on this job, what you need to know is how much money you will earn after accounting for your expenses. Although this is not a pricing decision, the concepts of incremental and irrelevant costs are still very useful to answer this question.

Imagine that you are looking for a second, part-time job and are considering driving for Uber or Lyft (or both)[8]. The requirements for this job are that you need to have a fairly new car, a driver's license, a clean driving record, and a smartphone.

Let's assume you own a late-model Ford Fusion car and an Android smartphone and are already making monthly payments of $375 for the car, and $65 for the phone and its service plan. Further, your comprehensive car insurance payment is $80 per month. Which of these costs should you consider in calculating how much money you will earn driving for Uber? At the first blush, you may wish to include all three payments, the monthly car payment, your smartphone payment, and your car insurance payment, and add your driver's license renewal fee to the mix. However, this would be wrong.

Because you know the concepts of incremental and irrelevant costs, it is clear that all three payments are recurring fixed costs. You will incur each of them regardless, whether you drive for Uber or Lyft, or not. These expenses are non-incremental and therefore irrelevant to the decision of whether to take on the driving gig. The only relevant expenses that should be considered are the cost of gasoline and the expense of your car's wear-and-tear from all the extra ride-share driving. You can go online and find out exactly how much this will cost you per mile of driving for your particular vehicle. For a late-model Ford Fusion, it is $0.48 per mile for operating the car[9]. This is the only incremental expense that matters and the one you should use when you are considering your net earnings from driving for Uber or Lyft. Strictly speaking, even the cost of your smartphone's battery usage is irrelevant. If you are like the rest of us, you will be using your smartphone anyway, whether you drive for Uber or not. So it does not count. Putting this idea in simpler terms: "*If you would spend the money anyway, then the expense is irrelevant, and should not be included it in your decision.*"

Now that we have established the distinction between incremental and irrelevant costs with these examples, and emphasized the need to first correctly identify and then consider only incremental costs in pricing decisions, we can move on to the idea of price floors in the *value pricing framework*.

COSTS SET THE FLOOR ON PRICE

To understand the price floor concept, let us consider the example of a cruise line that operates a cruise ship. It is trying to decide on its cabin pricing for one particular week-long Caribbean cruise. Imagine that this cruise ship incurs fixed costs of $50 per cabin per night and variable costs of $10 per cabin per night for the cruise. Its fixed costs include such things as the cost of the ship's lease, port fees to berth in the ports of call, wages paid to the crew, entertainers, housekeeping, maintenance, back-office staff, and other cruise ship employees[10]. These fixed costs remain the same regardless of the occupancy rate for the week-long cruise. Variable costs, on the other hand, change with the occupancy rate, or the number of guests on the cruise. Variable costs include the costs of food, amenities, cooling of occupied cabins, laundering sheets, per-passenger port costs, if any, and travel agent commissions.

THE DISTINCTION BETWEEN LONG-TERM AND SHORT-TERM PRICE FLOORS

For the cabin pricing decision, the cruise ship's fixed costs and variable costs set two different floors on what it can charge its guests. Over the course of the year, the cruise line company must charge an average minimum price of $60 per cabin per night to its customers. We can call this the "long-term price floor" for the cabin pricing decision. This is a hard "survival" metric of pricing performance. If the cruise liner does not meet this minimum threshold, it will eventually have to stop sailing in the Caribbean and find a permanent port of call (a.k.a. bankruptcy). The average long-term price of a product must cover both fixed and variable costs, which leads to the following truism: *Total costs establish the long-term price floor on the product's price.*

However, in the short-run, the pricing decision is starkly different. Let's say I decide I want to go on the Caribbean cruise two days before its sail date. It turns out that the ship is only half-full at this point. What should the cruise line charge me for my cabin? One alternative is to stick to the $60 per night threshold and charge me a price that is higher than this amount. However, the cruise line will be well advised to consider asking me for a much lower price than $60 per night.

This is because, in the short-run, the cruise ship has already incurred or will incur the fixed costs no matter how many people go on this particular cruise. There is no way to get out of spending this money, so these costs are irrelevant. For this particular pricing decision of making me an offer to sail in two days, it only has to worry about covering its variable costs, which are the costs that are incremental to the pricing decision. Any price they offer me over $10 per night will still be a profitable price for them.

The incremental costs set the short-term price floor for pricing decisions. Remember, the cruise ship will sail in two days regardless, and the cabin they would assign me will sail empty if I do not sign on. So the cruise line might as well fill one cabin with me, covering the $10 per day of variable costs they will incur by having me on board. Consider how smart this move is. By offering a low last-minute price, they are opening the door to the possibility that I will spend money during the cruise on high-margin services such as buying alcoholic drinks, gambling in the casino, and so on. This in turn will earn them additional revenue and contribute to covering the fixed costs, or perhaps even flow to its bottom line. A short-term price floor brings this creativity to pricing decisions. It arises from the fact that the company has a much lower threshold to overcome. From this example, our lesson is:

> **Incremental costs establish the short-term price floor on the product's price. Short-term price floors, if used creatively and judiciously, create significant customer value, growing the business while maintaining or increasing profit levels, and benefit the company's financial performance.**

Short-term price floors provide managers with lots of flexibility in their pricing strategy. When a company already has a stable base of regular customers who buy its products or services at full prices, and it still has spare capacity available, it can use the short-term price floor to design any number of creative and highly profitable offers. These offers can attract new customers, encourage product trial, reward regular customers, and build stronger relationships. Here are some creative uses of the short-term price floor:

- Luxury hotels routinely sell empty rooms at the last minute for a fraction of the regular price on sites like Priceline or Hotwire. As examples, using the "Name Your Own Price" feature on Priceline in January 2017, last-minute travelers snagged a room in the Westin Park Central Dallas for $61 (regularly priced at $169) and at Houston's J.W. Marriott Galleria for $71 (regular priced room at $299)[11]. The hotels continue to attract their core base of business travelers and fill empty rooms with price-sensitive clientele who do not mind waiting until the last minute, in effect stealing customers away from moderately priced competitors.

- Many Broadway shows sell any remaining available seats through sites like TodayTix or the TKTS discount booths in New York City on the day of the performance for much lower than regular prices. Those who want to see the show would never settle for the uncertainty. This approach draws new patrons into the empty seats.

- Even the most popular and buzzworthy restaurants offer great deals on food and drink during happy hour (usually 4–6 pm). Uchi is a well-liked restaurant in Houston and is sold out for dinner, weeks in advance. It offers happy hour appetizer plates for $3–6, and drinks for $3–7[12]. These prices are significantly lower than its regular prices and are designed to cover its incremental costs while bringing in new customer segments with champagne tastes and beer budgets (or sushi tastes and tilapia budgets) during slow periods of the day[13].

- The Tricycle Theater in Kilburn England uses Pay What You Want (PWYW) pricing for certain tickets and performances. Customers can buy tickets and pay anything they want for them. These PWYW tickets are only available for certain performances at the theater, and even then they can be purchased only on the day of the event, not in advance. This allows the theater to sell its tickets at the regular price to its core customer base of theatergoers, and fill any remaining seats with thrifty people who will buy PWYW tickets for last-minute seats at lower than regular prices.

In each of these cases, the organization has multiple goals. It wants to generate additional revenue by filling unused capacity with a much lower price floor. At the same time, it intends to capitalize on the flexibility in pricing afforded by the lower baseline to introduce its products to new customer segments or to test new product ideas in ways that benefit the high-priced core sales. One word of caution: these creative offers are only meant to work at the margins, to fill left-over capacity that would otherwise be wasted. They should never take the place of the core marketing activities that design and make compelling full-priced offers to the company's established customer base.

THE COST-BASED PRICING METHOD

Cost-based pricing is the Kardashian of the pricing world, widely ridiculed yet tremendously popular. Every manager claims to hate this practice and scoffs at it. With its different variations, cost-based pricing remains the most widely used pricing method in companies and non-profit organizations today. Most government and large B2B buyers use or mandate some variation of cost-based pricing. For instance, one large infrastructure services company that I know bids for multi-year, multi-billion dollar contracts that require quoted prices to be explicitly based on costs.

The cost-based pricing method is standard in the retailing industry as well, where the retailer may use a rule of thumb such as "double markup" to mark up the wholesale cost of merchandise by 100% to calculate its price. In the restaurant industry, consultants and industry veterans often have established benchmarks, such as food should be marked up by 2X, and beverages and bar should be marked up by 3X-5X[14].

MARKUP PRICING AND COST-PLUS PRICING

Contrary to popular understanding, distinct variations of cost-based pricing methods are used in different industries. While the general principle of calculating costs and then multiplying them by a chosen markup factor is common, the costs to be included in the calculation and how they are allocated to each unit of the product differ.

In the markup pricing method that is commonly used for consumer products and services such as restaurants and retailers, the company chooses a markup factor that is conventionally used in the industry and applies it only to the variable cost of the product that is being sold. For example, a bar may buy bottled beer from its supplier by the case at the cost of $0.85 per bottle. To price it for sale, it may use a markup factor of five (5X) because it is conventional for bars to do so. Its price for the beer will then be $0.85 x 5, or $4.25 per bottle. With this method, markup factors tend to be higher than they are with cost-plus pricing because they are applied only to the variable portion of the company's costs and have to cover all costs, including fixed costs.

In business markets, the cost-plus pricing method (also known as full-cost pricing) is more common[15]. The essential difference between cost-plus pricing and markup pricing is that cost-plus pricing considers all costs, not just variable costs in the calculation. With this method, in addition to variable costs, the company calculates all fixed costs that it expects to incur and allocates them to products in computing prices. Let's use a concrete example to illustrate how the cost-plus pricing method works.

Imagine a small pharmaceutical company that has spent $1 million in R&D costs to develop a new drug. It is submitting a bid to supply the government with 1,000,000 doses, its entire annual production of this drug. To produce these doses, the company will incur $500,000 in fixed costs, and $1 per dose of variable costs to produce and distribute this drug. The contracting process calls for using cost-plus pricing and a markup factor of 20%. In this scenario, here's how the calculation of the cost-plus price works out.

Fixed costs	= $1,000,000 (R&D) + $500,000
Total fixed costs	= $1,500,000
Number of doses	= 1,000,000
Allocated fixed costs per dose	= $1.5
Variable costs per dose	= $1.0
Total costs per dose	= $2.5
Markup stipulated in contract	= 20%
Price per dose	= $2.5*1.20 = $3.0

Figure 4.1 Cost-plus pricing calculation

Compared to markup pricing, cost-plus pricing is more difficult to use because it requires more assumptions. The company has to first estimate all its fixed costs for a period of time in advance. Then it has to predict how many units of product it will sell over that period. Only then can it calculate the fixed costs to be allocated to each product. The markup factor used in cost-plus pricing is typically lower than the one used in markup pricing because it is applied to all costs, fixed and variable, and not just variable costs.

Further, notice that in the calculation in Figure 4.1, we have allocated all R&D costs ($1,000,000) to the government contract. If the drug is sold in other markets or to other customer segments, then the company will have to judge about how much of the R&D costs to allocate to the government contract. This will lower the cost-based price correspondingly. Depending on this allocation (and the assumptions behind it), the quoted price could change significantly.

THE BENEFITS OF COST-BASED PRICING

Now that we know how the two main variations of the cost-based pricing method work, we can examine its pros and cons. This will help you decide whether cost-based pricing is suitable for your company.

1) It is simple. As the examples illustrate, cost-based pricing is relatively simple to use. Any retail frontline employee or bartender with a calculator can apply a markup factor of 2X or 5X to wholesale costs and calculate the price to charge customers in a store or bar.

2) It is easy to explain and justify. In addition to being simple, the cost-based method can be described and defended easily to employees and customers. Because of a long history of use in companies, everyone is familiar with the logic behind markups. The cost-based pricing method offers a reasonable explanation for why prices are what they are. For example, there is an inherent logic of fairness in telling customers, "We mark up the merchandise in our store by 50% to cover our costs and to earn a reasonable profit so we can stay in business, create jobs, and support our community."

3) It stabilizes market prices. When all the key competitors in a market have similar cost structures, and they all use cost-based pricing, the amount of risk associated with pricing decisions is lowered for everyone. Prices remain stable, particularly when the higher-cost suppliers in the market offer higher-quality products and lower-cost providers offer lower-quality products. Companies are less likely to engage in price wars if they base their prices primarily on costs instead of competitors' prices. (However, this can change when one competitor has an advantageous cost structure).

4) It encourages customers to use non-price factors in their decision making. For consumers, cost-based prices are consistent with expectations. Most of us expect to find lower service quality with low prices to match when we walk into an Aldi or Walmart store, and higher service quality and more upscale and expensive products in Whole Foods. Because of this pattern, in an industry that primarily uses cost-based prices, customers will base their purchase decisions on the product's quality rather than on its prices.

There is a gritty common sense and logic associated with cost-based pricing that is hard to dispute. However, if this is the case, why do so many managers and practically every pricing expert on the planet hate cost-based pricing?

THE LIMITATIONS OF COST-BASED PRICING

For most organizations, there are significant disadvantages to relying strictly on a cost-based pricing method for pricing decisions. Some reasons are obvious, but others are a little more complicated. Let us consider each one.

1) It encourages inefficiency. Cost-based pricing violates a core principle of good management practice, which is that increases in efficiency and productivity are good for everyone, company and customers alike. With cost-based pricing, there is a disincentive for companies to be efficient and to lower costs. Other things being equal, with this method, reducing costs will decrease company revenues and total profits. In contrast, increasing costs will raise prices, boosting revenues and profit.

Business consultant Anna Masker described a time when she worked with a B2B company that used cost-plus pricing to quote prices for complex industrial jobs. One year, when the business changed its manufacturing process and generated significant savings in labor costs, "the [pricing] system used the cost-plus model, so with lower costs, the final price was lower, ultimately passing all the cost savings on to customers. For this company, it meant hundreds of thousands of dollars of lost revenue—and profit[16]." Any pricing method that encourages inefficiencies, rewards bloated cost structures, and penalizes efficient, lean ones, has serious fundamental problems.

2) It is divorced from customer value or reference prices. Cost-based pricing completely ignores the three other decision inputs from the *value pricing framework*. This can be dangerous, and in some cases, even fatal for the business. Consider a home brewer who has just spent a tremendous amount of his effort and money in developing and fine-tuning a pale ale beer recipe, and obtaining the requisite licenses to sell his product. He whips up a batch of his beer to sell at a music festival. Because of his small scale, and specialized ingredients, his total costs come out to $7 per 20 oz. bottle of beer. If this entrepreneur were to use cost-based pricing and mark up his costs by a reasonable 40%, he would end up with a price of $10 per bottle for his pale ale. How successful do you think his venture would be when beer drinkers can find an excellent glass of pale ale for less than half that price? As this example illustrates, unless the customer's economic valuation of the product and prices of other comparable products are taken into account, the pricing decision may end up being completely off-base.

3) It creates a false sense of complacency. When I ask a manager or entrepreneur why they use cost-based pricing, a typical response is some version of, "We cannot lose with this method. At a minimum, it is guaranteed to cover our costs." This is perhaps the most dangerous misconception about cost-based pricing of all.

To see why this is the case, let us return to the pharmaceutical company example summarized in Figure 4.1. Now, instead of the expected 1,000,000 doses of the drug, let's assume that the firm was only able to deliver 500,000 doses due to an ingredient shortage. Recall the price per dose was set at $3, based on total cost estimates of $2.50 per dose and a markup of 20%.

Because of lower sales, the company will now have to allocate its fixed costs over the smaller actual sales base. While the estimated fixed costs, based on sales of 1,000,000 doses were $1.5 per dose ($1,500,000/1,000,000), the real fixed costs will be $3 per dose ($1,500,000/500,000). Adding the variable costs of $1 per dose, the company will have spent a total of $4/dose to fulfill its contract and supply the drug. Because the contracted price is

$3 per dose, set at the beginning of the contract, the company will end up losing $1 per dose, or a total of $500,000 from this sale.

As this example illustrates, cost-based prices provide no guarantee of covering costs or earning a profit for the company. Because sales volume has to be guesstimated beforehand and fixed costs are allocated based on this forecast, they can be either too high or too low depending on how many units are sold. This, in turn, can lead to prices that are too low, or too high, respectively. Cost-based pricing can easily result in a devastating loss; like everything else in life, there is no guarantee with this method.

In the *value pricing framework*, conducting a cost-based pricing analysis is fine. However, the resulting price should be used as one input of many into the pricing decision, not the only input.

WHEN DOES COST-BASED PRICING WORK? THE CASES OF COSTCO AND EVERLANE

So far in this chapter, we have made a strong case against using cost-based pricing alone to make pricing decisions. However, it is not difficult to find companies that have been extremely successful using this method. In fact, cost leadership is one of the most popular business strategies in existence. This brings us to the second role of costs in the *value pricing framework*. It is to serve as the centerpiece of the firm's marketing strategy. When the company has constructed a business model or has unique competencies that allow it to have an advantageous cost structure relative to its competitors, it can use this asset to create and deliver one of the most enticing value propositions of all. In such cases, the company becomes a cost leader, and low costs, low prices, and superior value form an integral part of its brand identity.

As we saw in Chapter 3, Costco is one example of a successful company that has built a business model and a strong position in the market based primarily on its costs. The cornerstone of its pricing approach is markup pricing. The company mandates that nothing in its store will be marked up by more than 14 percent (15 percent for its private label products). It widely publicizes its markup pricing policy in its investor and industry presentations.

Markup pricing is advantageous for Costco because of two main reasons. The first reason is that it is the core of its positioning strategy. The visibility of low markup rates and the resulting low prices when compared to its competitors, when coupled with other value-oriented cues such as its warehouse-like store environment, limited assortments, and requirements to buy in bulk, create a powerful image that the customer is going to get great deals at Costco. Millions of customers find this value proposition to be irresistible. The second reason is that Costco's markup approach is part of a smart, two-pronged pricing approach where customers have to buy an annual membership to be able to shop at Costco. The membership fee, essentially an entrance fee, provides another substantial revenue stream and bulks up Costco's profits. Even though Costco's pricing method appears to be simple markup pricing, it camouflages a more sophisticated and carefully crafted strategic pricing approach that creates a differentiated and compelling value proposition for its customers.

A company does not need to be a cost leader to use cost-based pricing successfully. Another firm that openly and proudly practices markup pricing is startup online retailer Everlane. The company claims the value proposition of "Radical Transparency," and its tagline is "Know your factories. Know your costs. Always ask why." For each product it sells, it wants its customers to know exactly how it calculated the price. For one of its bestselling products, the Slim Fit Chambray Shirt, for example, the breakdown of costs is given as follows: Materials = $9.34, hardware (zippers, buttons, etc.) = $1.64, labor = $12.55, duties = $4.64, and transport = $0.60. The costs add up to $29, and they are marked up by 100% for a price of $58.

For purposes of comparison, the labor costs for a typical $14 garment made in Bangladesh are $0.12 (or less than 1% of the price)[17]. In sharp contrast, Everlane's labor costs of $12.55 comprise 22 percent of the $58 price tag, two orders of magnitude greater than the typical garment. Because this cost information and break-down are so readily provided, customers can verify Everlane's emphasis on paying fair wages to workers who manufacture its garments and can actively choose to endorse this company value by buying its products. In this case, markup pricing exposes the company's core values. Just like Costco, the company's entire business strategy supports and in turn, is bolstered by, its cost-based pricing method. No other pricing method would work as well, and none would align so well with Everlane's core value proposition of radical transparency.

Both Costco and Everlane are examples of companies where their cost inputs strongly drive pricing. Both companies are exemplars of the *value pricing framework*. They have given weight to costs because it aligns with their respective value propositions, and made cost-based pricing the centerpiece of their business strategy. They have used their pricing approach to create compelling and attractive offers for their core customers. Their prices reflect the value customers ascribe to their products.

These exceptions, however, prove the rule. While cost-based pricing provides useful indicators of sustainable prices, it is only successful when it is woven carefully with the company's marketing strategy, and reinforces its value proposition to target customers in a compelling and differentiated way.

Chapter Summary

In this chapter, we saw that costs are an important input and play two significant roles in pricing decisions. First, they set the floor or the lower bound on what prices the company can charge sustainably. Over the long-term, the company must comfortably cover all its costs if it wants to stay in business. However, over the short-term, for a well-established company with a solid base of regular customers, the threshold of costs is much lower. It only has to cover its variable costs, and can use this flexibility to design and make creative offers to use its spare capacity, attract new customers, and strengthen current customer relationships.

The second role of costs is to serve as the cornerstone of the firm's marketing strategy. When the company has a cost advantage, it can use its superior or unique cost structure to attract like-minded customers, and develop a strong brand identity that is centered around costs. We also saw that, while cost-based pricing provides useful estimates of potentially suitable prices, it should never be the only method used to make pricing decisions. Knowing costs fully and understanding how they change with prices and customer demand will allow you to design effective pricing policies for your organization.

[5]

CUSTOMER VALUE

Do you have any idea what a man who wants Viagra would really pay for a pill if the opportunity suddenly arose, or needed to arise? – John Schwartz

In describing the idiosyncrasies of pricing in the cruise line industry, consultant Warren Lieberman tells an engaging story about how cruise liners priced cabins with balconies when they were first introduced on cruise ships in the 1990s[1]. Today, of course, we expect to pay a hefty premium for a cabin with a balcony. The balmy sea breezes, the light, and the sense of openness are all worth paying extra for, so customers will routinely pay 20%, 30%, or even more for a balcony. A higher price is aligned with greater customer value.

However, when balconies were first introduced on cruise ships, cabins that had balconies received a price cut. Their prices were lowered and they cost less than interior cabins. The managers used "square foot logic" for this pricing decision. Because balconies took up some of the original cabin space, cabin size shrank when balconies were added. Interior cabins now had greater square footage. Therefore, the managers reasoned that they should have higher prices. In making this pricing decision, the managers gave 100 percent weight to the cabin's dimensions, and zero weight to the sea breezes, the light, the sense of openness and the views afforded by the balcony.

If you're like me, such a pricing scheme and the logic underlying it will seem ludicrous. This reaction is because the pricing completely ignores customer valuation of the cruise ship cabin's features. The square foot logic bypasses the common sense that most cruise-goers will only be too happy to sacrifice cabin space, and pay a hefty premium for the experience that the balcony enables. According to Lieberman, it took the industry several years to recognize the flaw in their square foot logic and change their pricing calculus to include customer value.

THE DEFINITION OF A PRODUCT

In the *value pricing framework*, after costs, customer value is the second input into pricing decisions. Its importance is reflected by its presence in the framework's name. Customer value must be considered in every pricing decision. On the face of it, the concept of customer value seems straightforward: Give customers what they want. If we think of customer value in these terms, it can be defined as "all the different ways in which the customer derives benefits from purchasing and using the product." But what are these ways and how should we measure them? How should measures of customer value be translated into good pricing decisions? These are difficult questions to answer, and for pricing, they are among the most significant. We will tackle them in this chapter.

Most pricing experts acknowledge that understanding customer value and translating it into dollars and cents is one of the hardest challenges in pricing. The difficulty arises from the fact that customer value is a nebulous concept that is unique to both customer and context. As a result, even after decades of thinking about these questions, marketers still debate how to measure it in a uniform way that applies to all customers, and how to use it to determine the product's price[2].

We will bypass these problems, by employing a very precise and unambiguous definition of customer value. Before we can define customer value, however, we first need to precisely define what we mean by the product. Stay with me as we untangle these commonly known but ambiguously understood concepts carefully, one step at a time. Here's the definition of product we will use in this book[3]:

> **The product is a bundle of features that provides quantifiable functional and hedonic benefits to the customer.**

BUNDLE OF FEATURES

Each word in this definition is important. Let's begin with the phrase "bundle of features." Take the example of a hotel room in a luxury hotel. Imagine it has a king-sized bed with a memory gel mattress. It also has Egyptian cotton bedding, an ensuite bathroom with marble floors, luxurious toiletries, a hair dryer, a coffee machine, a flat panel TV, a mini-bar, a delicious room-service menu that is available 24 hours a day, and many other features.

What is more, the hotel has a well-equipped fitness center, attached parking, highly rated on-site restaurants, and a gourmet coffee shop in the lobby. It is also in a very desirable location, within walking distance of the city's convention center.

Together, this formidable bundle of features constitutes the "hotel room" product. When we describe the hotel room as a bundle of features, the following characteristics of the features are worth noting:

- The hotel room has an indeterminately large number of features. It has many other features I did not mention such as an attractive and durable carpet, a pillow menu, and a turndown service every evening. We could go on and on.

- Each time the hotel adds a new feature to the room, it incurs costs. Depending on the feature, these costs could be fixed (e.g., a Matisse print in the room), or variable (e.g., a bowl of fresh fruit delivered to the room each time a new guest checks in).

- The hotel room has many features in common with competitors' hotel rooms. For example, most luxury hotel rooms have an ensuite bathroom, branded toiletries, 24-hour room service, and on-site restaurants.

- Very few of its features are truly unique. For instance, the hotel may become the first one to provide a high-end espresso machine to guests in its rooms. Other luxury hotels, however, will quickly copy this amenity, especially if customers rave about it on TripAdvisor. Similarly, the hotel will adopt its competitors' successful new features.

These observations about product features generalize to every product and service, whether it is the latest Samsung television, an electric bicycle, a hospital ventilator, or an oil rig. In every case, the pricing challenge is to understand how the bundle of features translates into customer value.

FUNCTIONAL AND HEDONIC BENEFITS

Let's consider the next part of the product's definition, which is that the product "provides quantifiable functional and hedonic benefits." The product's features, individually and in combination, provide benefits to the customer. In fact, the translation of product features into benefits lies at the heart of good marketing practice. Novice marketers think of products in terms of product features, savvy ones think in terms of customer benefits. Over the years, marketing experts have developed many different typologies of customer benefits that can be applied to pricing decisions[4]. The typology we will use in the *value pricing framework* is simple, flexible, and practical. It classifies customer benefits into two fundamental types: *functional benefits* and *hedonic benefits*.

The first type, the product's functional benefits refer to benefits that the customer derives from the product's performance and is related to its core purpose[5]. When staying in a hotel room, for example, the functional benefits derived by the guest include having a safe place to stay and being able to sleep peacefully in a quiet and comfortable environment. These are the basic functions of every hotel room. They are the essence of what a hotel room is supposed to do. It is supposed to be safe, quiet, and comfortable. Is it surprising that guests find noisy or unsafe hotel rooms to be intolerable[6]?

Functional benefits can be described in terms that apply to many different products and services. Such functional benefits include "saves time," "provides variety," "reduces effort," "integrates" and "connects" in consumer markets, and "saves money," "reduces risk," "reduces costs," and "connects" in business markets[7].

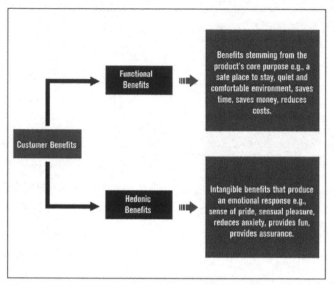

Figure 5.1 Functional and hedonic benefits delivered by the product

The second fundamental type of benefits that a product provides is hedonic benefits. These refer to benefits that are indirect, intangible and emotion producing. For the hotel guest, such benefits may include a sense of pride from staying in a luxury hotel, the sensual pleasure of sleeping on a memory gel mattress with soft Egyptian cotton sheets, the thrill of making friends and colleagues envious by posting photos of the luxurious room on Instagram, and so on. As marketing scholars have observed, hedonic benefits are associated with the customer's affective and sensory experiences, and specifically to the aesthetic or sensual pleasure derived from the consumption, and the sense of fantasy and fun that the product or service provides[8]. Bain consultants include "reduces anxiety," "makes me nostalgic," "increases wellness," "is fun," and "provides status" among the most common and widely sought-after types of hedonic benefits by customers.

When we describe the hotel room in terms of the functional and hedonic benefits it delivers, the following characteristics of the benefits are worth noting:

- Every customer derives benefits only from a subset of the hotel room's features. For instance, someone who does not watch television will derive no benefit from the state-of-the-art TV in the room. To this person, it is an irrelevant feature. Others may not order room service, not partake of the minibar, and so on, deriving zero value from these features, respectively.

- Complicating things even further, different customers derive benefits from different feature sets. One guest may use the hotel's fitness center and relish the room's quiet environment; another guest may order room service and watch TV, and so on. What is more, even the same feature will deliver different amounts of functional and hedonic benefits to different guests. For a fitness enthusiast, being able to work out in a well-equipped gym will be a sensual experience, delivering hedonic benefits. However, for a customer who sees working out as a necessary drudgery, the gym will have a purely functional value. Stated differently, every customer receives the same feature set but derives different types and amounts of benefits. This is a fundamental challenge with measuring customer value and translating it into the price.

Customer Value

Having covered the necessary background, we can describe customer value in this way: *The product's value is the sum total of all functional and hedonic benefits derived by the customer from the product's bundle of features.*

While this definition helps us understand the product's value from the customer's perspective, it still doesn't describe customer value in economic terms from the company's standpoint. Table 5.1 provides a summary of how leading pricing experts define customer value.

James Anderson, Nirmalya Kumar and James Narus	Value in business markets is the worth in monetary terms of the technical, economic, service, and social benefits a customer firm receives in exchange for the price it pays for a market offering.
Walter Baker, Michael Marn, and Craig Zawada	The true essence of value reflects the tradeoff between the benefits a customer receives from a product and the price paid for it—or, more accurately, the perceived benefits a customer receives and the perceived price paid. In other words, value equals perceived benefits minus perceived price. (p.46)
Russell Winer	Customer or perceived value is a measure of how much a customer is willing to pay for a product or service. (p.4)
Kent Monroe	Perceived value represents a trade-off between buyers' perceptions of quality and sacrifice and is positive when perceptions of quality are greater than perceptions of sacrifice. (p. 104)
Thomas Nagle and Joseph Zale	A product's total economic value is calculated as the price of the customer's next best alternative (the reference value) plus the worth of whatever differentiates the offering from the alternative (the differentiation value). (p. 19)
Reed Holden and Mark Burton	Financial value refers to profits that result when costs are subtracted from revenues. In a business-to-business context, dollars that fall to the customer's bottom line when it uses your offering is the true measure of financial value. (p. 24)

Tony Cram	Value is a combination of product (or service) performance, plus an emotional association. (p. 11).
Julie Meehan, Michael Simonetto, Larry Montan, and Christopher Goodin	Value refers to the importance or usefulness of a product or service to a specific customer or group of customers... It correlates closely with the various benefits a buyer receives from a specific offering and its features. In some cases, though, value can reflect an emotional or irrational response to an intangible element such as a brand name that has a special cachet. (p. 45).
Hermann Simon	The price a customer is willing to pay, and therefore the price a company can achieve, is always a reflection of the perceived value of the product or service in the customer's eyes. If a customer perceives a higher value, his or her willingness to pay rises. The converse is equally true: if the customer perceives a lower value relative to competitive products, willingness to pay drops. (p. 13).

Table 5.1 Definitions of customer value by leading pricing experts

Two common themes emerge from this set of definitions. First, most of them define customer value in financial or economic terms. "Willingness to pay" is a core concept in many of these definitions. For instance, both Russell Winer and Hermann Simon define customer value simply as how much money the customer is willing to pay for the product. The second common theme is the idea of a trade-off or exchange, which is that the customer gives up or sacrifices something, usually money, in return for the product's benefits.

ECONOMIC VALUE SHOULD BE QUANTIFIABLE

These two common themes in company-centered definitions of customer value bring us to the final piece of the product's definition that requires further elaboration. That is the word "quantifiable." For pricing decisions using this book's *value pricing framework*, the functional and hedonic benefits derived by the customer must be quantifiable. Our mantra is, *if you cannot quantify it, you cannot use it for pricing.* To appreciate this point, let's conduct a thought experiment.

Imagine that the hotel wants to increase the value it delivers to its guests. There's one guaranteed way to accomplish this: add more and more features to the room: Plush bathrobes. A rocking chair. A mini-library of current best-selling books. A limited-edition Matisse art print. A heated toilet seat. An iPad to use during the stay. And so on.

Even if this thought is tempting to us as customers, from the manager's perspective, we can quickly see just how infeasible such feature addition is. Every new feature costs money. More features provide greater customer benefits and value, but they also increase costs. This is where the notion of "quantifiable" benefits comes into play. It concretizes the trade-off involved in providing benefits to the customer and incurring costs to do so.

Functional and hedonic benefits have to be translatable into economic value, measured in dollars and cents. Specifically, the hotel can only provide features that the customer is willing to pay for. Bain consultant Eric Almquist observes, "The trick is to determine what elements to add in order to boost the perceived value of your offering. You don't want to expend resources adding features that consumers don't care about[9]." In this quotation, what Almquist means by "don't care about" is "aren't willing to pay for." The pricing view of customer value advanced in this book is that when customers care about a feature, they should be prepared to pay for it.

This point is not only necessary for designing and improving new products, but also for making good pricing decisions. The fundamental economic exchange proposition between the company and the customer, "We will offer you a bundle of features that deliver functional and hedonic benefits, and you should be willing to pay for them" is the essence of customer value in the *value pricing framework.*

Having understood these concepts, we are now ready to formally define customer value and consider its role in pricing decisions. As should be clear to you, the definition will depend upon whether customer value is defined from the client's perspective or the company's perspective.

> For a customer: Customer value is the sum total of all functional and hedonic benefits derived from the product's bundle of features.

Notice this customer-centered definition makes no mention of economic value or willingness to pay. It states that for a customer, adding more features to the product equates to greater functional and hedonic benefits, and to a greater value. Firmly tongue in cheek, I want you to think of your customer as a giant gluttonous seal with an endless appetite who keeps devouring every feature that is offered. In theory, every feature is additive to the value derived by the customer, without an upper limit.

However, this is obviously not the case when we define customer value from the company's perspective. In this definition, the customer's willingness to pay features prominently.

> For a company: Customer value is the total amount of money that the customer is willing to pay for the functional and hedonic benefits received by the product's bundle of features.

These dual definitions of customer value provide us with a critical insight for making pricing decisions. The product's price is nothing more and nothing less than the conversion of customer value into a monetary amount that the customer is willing to pay.

DOES ADDING PRODUCT FEATURES INCREASE CUSTOMER VALUE?

When companies are unclear about which definition of customer value they should be using, things can go very wrong. If they endorse and follow the customer-centric definition, they may add too many new features into the product with the idea that every customer will find something they like. Without a proper understanding of whether these features will translate into economic value for customers, this approach can lead to what pricing consultants Madhavan Ramanujam and Georg Tacke call "feature shock." According to them, feature shock reduces customer value rather than enhancing it, increasing the product's cost and price to untenable levels[10].

Smart companies, on the other hand, choose features strategically, providing explicit trade-offs to customers. Commerce Bank, at one time the fastest growing retail bank in the United States, positioned itself as the most convenient bank in the country by staying open seven days a week and maintaining longer hours than its peers. However, this feature was delivered with an explicit trade-off, as it paid out substantially lower interest rates on customer deposits. As marketing experts Frances Frei and Anne Morriss point out "The additional capital this choice generated gave the company the resources to fund better hours. In other words, convenient hours and lower rates were inextricably linked. Commerce could deliver excellence in hours precisely because of its dismal deposit rates[11]."

For effective pricing, customer value must be defined in economic terms and grounded in the philosophy that the company can only deliver features that the customer is willing to pay for.

MAPPING CUSTOMER BENEFITS TO ECONOMIC VALUE

To include customer value as a decision input in pricing decisions, we need a systematic method to translate the benefits derived by customers into economic value earned by the company. The customer value grid provides one method to quantify customer value. Using a survey-based approach, it employs the following four steps:

Step 1): Unbundle the product into its constituent features.

Step 2): Understand the hedonic and functional benefits derived by customers from each product feature. (For this step, it is important to choose a sample of customers from the target segment).

Step 3): Ask customers to quantify the benefits in economic terms, that is, how much they are willing to pay for each benefit.

Step 4): Add the economic value of each benefit to calculate the product's total economic value to the customer. This is the customer value input into the pricing decision.

Let's use the hotel room example to illustrate how this method works. Figure 5.2 shows the customer value grid for the hotel room. It sequentially connects the hotel room's features, the resulting benefits, and the economic value that the customer is willing to pay for the benefits.

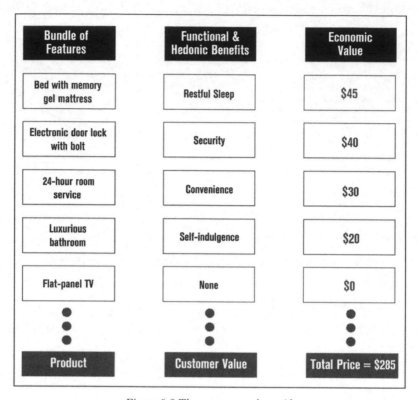

Figure 5.2 The customer value grid

Every product feature leads to a potential customer benefit, which in turn leads to a potential increase in economic value. In the figure, the hotel customer values a bed with a memory gel mattress because it provides restful sleep, and is willing to pay $45 for the benefit. The electronic door lock with the bolt is worth $40 to the customer because it provides security, but the flat panel TV is worth nothing because the customer does not watch television. Once the economic value of all the features and benefits is tallied up, it comes to $285. This includes features not shown in Figure 5.2.

HOW TO DEVELOP AND INTERPRET A CUSTOMER VALUE GRID

In its simplest form, the four steps of the customer value grid are conducted by asking questions with a survey. Methods that are more sophisticated capture the tradeoffs between benefits and price directly. The most widely used of these methods is conjoint analysis. Further, to increase the grid's usefulness, the following tips about its implementation may be useful to you.

1) In reality, every product has an indeterminate number of features. However, for practical purposes, it is important to reduce the set to the approximately ten features that are deemed the most important. Alternatively, if your interest is in introducing a new feature to the product, it should be the focus of the survey.

2) Although you may be tempted to skip the benefits questions and go straight from features to economic value by asking questions such as "How much would you be willing to pay for a bed with a memory gel mattress?" or "How much would you be willing to pay for 24-hour room service?" resist this temptation. The intermediate step of asking about the benefits derived from each product make it easier for customers to translate features into economic value.

3) Getting customers to provide a dollar amount for each benefit can be a challenge. Because the survey is conducted by the company, there is an inherent conflict of interest involved. Customers would rather provide low-ball estimates to keep prices low. This conflict can be averted by using survey-based methods that measure the trade-offs between benefits and economic value directly.

4) The price obtained from the value grid exercise will be different for each customer. In a consumer market, responses from a broad cross-section of 300-400 respondents belonging to a target segment should be obtained. These responses can be averaged to get a sense of which features provide the greatest benefits and economic value, and to calculate an average price for the segment. In a business market, the value grid can be done for individual customer accounts or customer segments with much smaller samples.

5) Just like the price derived from cost-based pricing, the price derived from this exercise is one input into making pricing decisions. It reflects the economic value that the customer places on the product, and forms the ceiling on prices the company can charge. However, it is neither the "best" price nor the "optimal" price for the product. In fact, as we will see later in this book, being able to earn the value grid-derived price may be infeasible or detrimental to the company for good reasons.

HOW CUSTOMERS TRADE-OFF PRICE AND QUALITY TO JUDGE VALUE: THE EMERY MODEL

Although the value grid is a useful way to measure customers' valuation of the product at the individual feature level, in reality, only the most careful and diligent customers will use such an elaborate method each time they purchase a product. The reason is simple. It is just too effortful and time-consuming to calculate and then aggregate the economic value of product features. People use more straightforward cognitive short-cuts to assess value on a day-to-day basis that relies on judging the trade-offs between the product's price and its quality.

When we considered the different ways in which pricing experts define customer value in Table 5.1 earlier in this chapter, the idea of a trade-off or exchange was a common theme in the definitions. Customers determine what they will give up or sacrifice (usually money) and the benefits they will receive from purchasing the product and the extent to which the sacrifice and the benefits are in the balance with each other.

Pricing expert Fred Emery developed a model in 1969[12] that provides a descriptive framework of this trade-off and value judgment process that is useful even today. The Emery model explains how consumers make judgments of value by considering both price and quality of the product. The model is graphically illustrated in figure 5.3.

The Emery model distinguishes between the objective quantities of price and quality and their subjective levels as perceived by the customer, which are then mapped to each other to form judgments of value. We will use the example of a LED light bulb to illustrate how the Emery model works.

Imagine a LED light bulb that is priced at $3. It is sold by a brand named Kangaroo that is unfamiliar to you. The bulb is 60W equivalent (consuming approximately 9 watts of electricity) and has a tested life of 20,000 hours. For the Emery model analysis, its objective quality is 20,000 hours of life, and its objective price is $3.

According to Emery, to assess the bulb's value, the customer does not use objective price and quality. Instead, by utilizing previous experience, knowledge about available prices and quality levels, and information obtained from sources such as product displays, websites, ads, and so on, the customer converts these objective values into subjective judgments of price and quality. In Emery's words, "price judgments are relative, not absolute; relative to what is known of other prices as well as being relative to the significance attached to the associated use-values."

Further, subjective judgments of customers are ordered categories. A customer may map a price of $1 (or less) as a cheap price for the LED bulb, around $3 as a reasonable price, and around $5 as a very high price (see left panel of Figure 5.3). Stated differently, when making judgments of value, and deciding whether to buy the product, the customer does not think in terms of actual prices, but in terms of subjective prices. The same is the case with quality. The customer will translate a tested life of 5,000 hours (the objective level of quality) into a subjective judgment of "bad quality" for the LED bulb, 10,000 hours into "average quality," and 20,000 hours into "excellent quality." If the customer has knowledge about the brand, it will serve to recalibrate the translations of objective quality into subjective quality. In other words, a well-known brand may be able to get away with a lower level of objective quality.

To assess the Kangaroo LED bulb's value, its subjective price is mapped onto its subjective quality and a comparison is made to arrive at the value. In our example, the $3–20,000-hour life LED light bulb will be seen as, "this bulb has a reasonable price, and it has excellent quality," which in turn will be translated as "this bulb is a good value." If the bulb were priced at $5 and had a tested life of only 5,000 hours, it would be "very expensive and poor quality." It would be interpreted as, "this bulb is poor value."

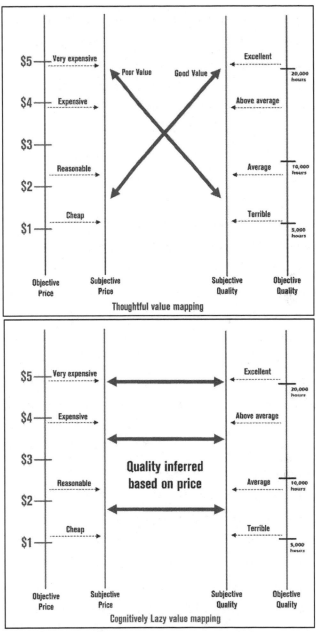

Figure 5.3 The Emery model: How customers trade-off price and quality to form judgments of value

The Emery model also explains how customers form judgments of a product's value when they are cognitively lazy, and rely on mental shortcuts instead of examining and mapping objective price and quality levels to subjective levels. In such cases, customers simply use the product's price to infer its quality. If the bulb's price is $5, for example, rather than learning its tested life, converting it to a subjective quality judgment and then mapping it to a subjective price, they will simply infer that the bulb must be of high quality (see bottom panel of Figure 5.3). On the other hand, if the bulb costs $1, it will be regarded as a poor quality bulb. Even in today's world where neuroscience and artificial intelligence are increasingly prevalent, the simplicity and descriptive power of the Emery model has important practical implications for every manager who is responsible for making effective pricing decisions. Let's consider three of the most important ones.

1) Rather than understanding the customer's willingness to pay for the product, the Emery model suggests that it is more useful to understand the customer's range of subjective prices. We will pursue this point in detail in the next chapter. For now, reverting to our hotel room example from earlier, the target customer may see prices below $50 as indicative of cheap hotel rooms, $51-100 as average priced, $101-200 as above average priced, and any room above $200 as expensive. The insight here is that customers are not as sensitive to specific prices as managers tend to think. They will be relatively unaffected by small price changes as long as they remain within the range of subjective price perception.

2) Understanding which objective quality metrics customers use to form their subjective judgments of quality is important information for the manager. When I purchased my Toyota Prius a few years ago, the vehicle's fuel-economy and Consumer Reports' rating of the car's reliability were both critical considerations for me. I combined these two objective measures of the Prius' quality to form my subjective judgment of quality. Once the manager understands which quality measures are important to the customer, they can take steps to manage quality perceptions, just as they do for price perceptions.

3) Perhaps the most insightful and thought-provoking idea from the Emery model is that customers will use different methods to map subjective price and quality judgments onto each other to form an assessment of the product's value, based on undertaking the evaluation thoughtfully versus using an inference or short-cut. When they use a shortcut, and use price to infer quality, high prices will contribute to a positive assessment of quality, and support rather than hinder judgments of customer value. On the other hand, cutting prices, or maintaining low prices may be viewed as a mark of poor quality, and hurt the product's sales. This is a crucial point that managers often overlook because it goes against the grain of their intuition.

Yet recent academic research provides more and more evidence to support this idea. Research on the "placebo pricing effect," for instance, shows that when a drug has a lower price, it actually works less effectively on consumers (who know its price). In one controlled experiment, 85 percent of the patients who thought they were taking an expensive pain relieving medicine (priced at $2.50 for each pill) reported a significant reduction in pain when they were administered electric shocks afterwards compared to only 61 percent for those who were taking cheaper pills that were discounted to 10 cents. In reality, everyone in the study took the same placebo pill[13]. Subjective judgments of price and quality are powerful determinants not only of perceived customer value but also of actual value derived from the product.

CHAPTER SUMMARY

In this chapter, we saw that customer value is a significant input into pricing decisions. Considering every product as a bundle of features, from the customer's perspective, customer value is the sum total of functional and hedonic benefits delivered by these features. The company's perspective is different. It focuses on the total amount of money the customer is willing to pay to receive the benefits, spelling out the trade-offs involved for customers between receiving greater benefits and having to pay more for them, or choosing which benefits are most important for a particular level of price. For pricing decisions, customer value reflects the economic value that the customer places on the product. Its primary role is to set the ceiling or an upper limit on prices that can be charged for the product.

We also studied the Emery model in this chapter, which describes how customers trade off levels of price and quality to form a judgment of the product's value. Instead of using objective levels of price and product quality in making this determination, customers convert these quantities into subjective judgments— low, average price, expensive, etc. for the price, and excellent, poor, terrible, etc. for quality. The customer then maps these subjective values of price and quality on to each other to arrive at a judgment of the product's value. The main implication of the Emery model is that customers' judgments of prices play a larger role in their decision making than actual numerical prices.

The key learning from this chapter is not to take customer value for granted or to assume its origins or amounts. You should probe diligently and understand which features of your product or service are important to the customer, how much they are willing to pay for them, and how they convert objective price and quality levels into subjective perceptions of value.

[6]

REFERENCE PRICES

Everything is relative, and only that is absolute. – Auguste Comte

Imagine Julie is at the grocery store and wants to buy a jar of peanut butter. As she considers her options, one particular brand on the store shelf stands out. It has attractive packaging, is made from organic peanuts grown on a local farm, and is endorsed by a celebrity chef. However, it is a brand Julie has not heard of, and is priced at $3.69.

Is this a good price for the peanut butter? If she is like most of us, Julie will find this question rather difficult to answer. By itself, the product's $3.69 price tag lacks a frame of reference, so it is unclear whether it is a good price. However, if she is informed that the average price of peanut butter in the store is $5, judging the brand's price may become a little easier for her. This additional information will provide Julie with a much-needed frame of reference, even if it is not the most appropriate frame.

Price Judgments Are Relative, Not Absolute

When customers make judgments about prices, they almost never make them in isolation. A product's price is judged in relation to other prices[1]. These other prices, known as reference prices, provide customers with frames of reference or benchmarks against which the product's price is assessed, and decisions are made about whether the price is too high, too low, or reasonable. This relative judgment of price, in turn, becomes an important factor in the customer's decision to purchase the product.

For the organization, the reference prices of customers provide one of the four main decision inputs in the *value pricing framework*. Reference prices play two important roles in the company's pricing strategy. First, knowing which prices customers use as reference prices gives insight into the range of prices that customers consider to be reasonable. For example, if Julie already has a frame of reference for peanut butter, and uses $3.99 (the price she paid last time), $5.39 (the price of the national brand) and $2.99 (the price of the store's private label brand) as three reference prices in judging the $3.69 price of the new peanut butter, $2.99–$5.39 will be Julie's range of reasonable prices. These are peanut butter prices Julie knows about and uses for comparison purposes. Once the range of reasonable prices is well understood, the company can strategically decide where it wants to price its products in relation to this range. Importantly, the information provided by customers' range of reasonable prices is a third unique data point for making good pricing decisions. Because it consists of prices of other comparable products, it provides a unique signal beyond those provided by costs (which sets the short and long-term floors on prices) and customer value (which sets the ceiling)[2].

While the first role of reference prices in the *value pricing framework* is informative, its second function is persuasive. The manager can "supply" a strategically chosen reference price to the customer to produce a favorable comparison for the product. For example, if the peanut butter, priced at $3.69, is placed on the grocery store shelf next to another brand that costs $4.79, it will appear to be a good deal simply by virtue of its location. However if it is displayed next to a brand that only costs $2.99, it will seem to be pricey even though nothing about it has changed. Another way to influence customers' price judgment is to supply a "normal" price. For instance, a shelf label for the peanut butter that says "Normal price = $4.69, Limited time sale price = $3.69" will also make the peanut butter appear to be a good deal because it is cheaper than its regular price. Marketers use a variety of such price cues to persuade customers and influence their behavior.

In this chapter, we will examine these two roles of reference prices in detail. Our goal is to understand how to use customers' reference prices to price effectively.

REFERENCE PRICES ESTABLISH THE RANGE OF REASONABLE PRICES

In the *value pricing framework*, the first role of reference prices is to set the frame of comparison and determine the customer's range of reasonable prices for the product. Academic pricing researchers make the distinction between internal and external reference prices that is very useful in understanding how reference prices work[3].

Internal reference prices are estimates about what the product should cost that customers already have in their heads. More formally, internal reference prices are defined as the prices the customer knows, believes, or expects the product to have based on their first-hand knowledge, past purchase experiences, and information obtained through advertisements, reviews, and word-of-mouth[4]. For example, when I go to buy a sandwich for lunch, I expect it to cost around $5. This is my internal reference price, formed over years of buying sandwiches. The "around $5" phrase is important because it captures the imprecision of internal reference prices. Internal reference prices are rarely single numbers. More often, they tend to be a range. In fact, it is quite common for customers to consider a range of prices to be acceptable or reasonable based on their prior knowledge of the product category. In our example, the "around $5 for a sandwich" reference price means that I consider a range of prices centered on $5, say between $4 and $6, to be reasonable for a sandwich.

Further, for the same product, customers usually have multiple internal reference prices that are dependent on its quality. Each reference price range is associated with a certain product quality level. Thus, in our example, while I consider $4-$6 as the reasonable price range for a sandwich, I do not mind spending much more, $10-$15, occasionally for a sit-down lunch in a nice restaurant. My acceptable price range is much lower, only $1-$2 when I want to grab a quick hot dog or a taco from a food truck.

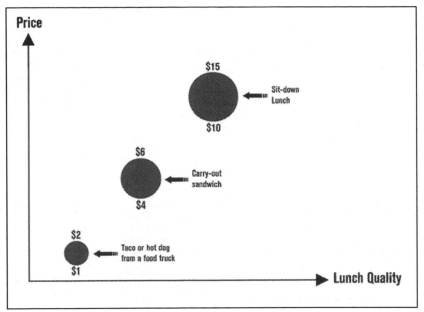

Figure 6.1. Range of reasonable prices vary with the product's quality level

Reasonable reference prices are rarely precise values and are usually a range for one important reason. Customers are notoriously poor at remembering, let alone using, specific prices when they make purchases. In a famous study conducted in 1990, marketing professors Peter Dickson and Alan Sawyer intercepted supermarket customers within seconds after they had selected and placed an item in their grocery cart, and asked them how much the item cost. Amazingly, less than half of those intercepted were able to recall the item's exact price[5]. In another 2002 study of French shoppers, only about 2% could remember exact prices, but around 33% could accurately spot whether the product's price was a deal[6]. These studies are consistent with the Emery model we studied in the last chapter. They show that customers are more likely to use price ranges rather than specific price values as frames of reference.

In the *value pricing framework*, the customer's range of reasonable prices for different quality levels of the product category is a critical piece of information. This range is used for making pricing decisions in three important ways.

1) THE RANGE OF REASONABLE PRICES PROVIDES THE PATH OF LEAST RESISTANCE FOR SETTING A GOOD PRICE.

Some marketers refer to the range of reasonable prices as "normative" prices[7] because these are prices that the customer expects to pay, and considers to be fair prices for the product. Once the company understands the target customer's range, setting or keeping the product's price within this range is tantamount to reducing or eliminating the significance of the product's price from the customer's purchase decision. Simply put, when a product is priced within the reasonable range, the price is less likely to be a hurdle to making the purchase.

Obviously, many, or even most customers may still not buy the product but their choice will be based on an assessment of the product's other attributes, not its price. Returning to the sandwich example, if I am offered a sandwich in the $4-6 range, I will consider characteristics such as the type of bread, the number and combination of ingredients, and the calories, in deciding whether to buy the sandwich. Its price will be insignificant in my decision because I have already deemed it as reasonable. The range of reasonable prices is a powerful concept for pricing decisions because it regulates the importance customers give to price relative to the product's other attributes.

2) CUSTOMERS ARE INSENSITIVE TO PRICE CHANGES WITHIN THE RANGE OF REASONABLE PRICES.

Another important upshot of customers' use of a reference price range instead of a single precise value is that they will be relatively insensitive to price changes as long as the "before" and "after" prices remain within the range. Where the company's pricing decisions are concerned, what makes this fact even more influential and important is that customers wrongly believe in their knowledge of prices, and think their ability to discern even minute changes is better than it really is[8]. Even after the price is changed, customers will continue to behave as if it has not changed. Savvy marketers exploit this customer bias to their advantage.

Among pricing experts, the range of reasonable prices goes by different names such as "the zone of indifference" and "the latitude of price acceptance[9]." Research shows that the range of reasonable prices varies considerably depending on both the product and the customer. In the original study where this concept was introduced, the range of reasonable prices for grocery products was found to be around 4 to 5% on each side of the product's average price, making the total range of reasonable prices around 10% of the category's average price. As an example, for the peanut butter we considered earlier, if the average price across all brands was $5, its range of reasonable prices for customers would be from $4.50 to $5.50. Other studies have shown that the range is far greater, as much as 15 to 20% for products that are discretionary purchases. The range also varies depending on the price magnitude as shown in Figure 6.1. For a small numerical price, the range is narrow. As the magnitude of price increases, the band increases correspondingly[10]. Figure 6.2 shows how this concept works in a graphical format.

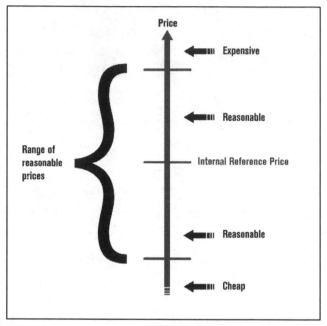

Figure 6.2 How customers use the range of reasonable prices to make price judgments

3) SHIFTING THE PRICE TO THE HIGH END OF THE RANGE OF REASONABLE PRICES IS AN EFFECTIVE PRICING STRATEGY.

Imagine your company sells the peanut butter that Julie was considering at the beginning of this chapter. You know that your target customers' range of reasonable prices for peanut butter is $4.50–$5.50. Where will you price your brand? The answer is that you would be better off by setting your price at the higher end of the range, say at $5.39 or $5.49, to earn the highest price and profit margin on your product. With these prices, you will remain within the range of reasonable prices and avoid any customer judgment that your peanut butter is expensive compared to your competition.

Companies such as Panera Bread, Chipotle, and Torchy's Tacos are adept at using their target customers' range of reasonable prices effectively. When pricing their menus, they deliberately price their items at substantially higher (and we would expect, more profitable) levels than competitors such as Taco Bell or McDonald's. For instance, Chipotle's burritos are priced at $6.50 to $7.50, well above the $3 to $5 range of Taco Bell[11]. These prices remain within the higher limit of reasonable prices for Chipotle's target customers so that they are more likely to use quality of ingredients, location, experience, and other factors in choosing which burrito to buy for lunch.

THE CASE OF THE DIGITAL MARKETING AGENCY

A digital marketing agency provides a portfolio of services to the healthcare industry. Its services include website design and maintenance, SEO, management of its clients' social media and email marketing programs, and app development. The agency wanted to enter a new customer segment and offer these services to medium-sized hospitals but did not have a good understanding of what prices would be reasonable for this particular customer segment. It had some pricing decisions to make, including the following big three decisions:

- Should each service be priced a la carte, or should they be bundled into a package of solutions?
- Should the price quote be given on an hourly basis by marking up labor costs (which were its main incremental costs) or

should a lump-sum price be quoted to the customer for the services?

- What prices should the company ask for?

In assessing how competitors priced their offerings to the medium-sized hospital segment, the marketing agency quickly discovered that virtually all the key players only offered solution packages. No one offered à la carte services. What is more, they all required annual contracts. The analysis also found that the range of reasonable prices for the medium-sized hospitals was much bigger, and centered on a much higher average than what the agency had thought or used for its existing customers in other healthcare segments.

Armed with this information, the company put together a pricing schedule for hospitals that was in line with competitor prices. It took care to remain within the clients' range of reasonable prices but priced its services a little higher than the average to create an aura of quality. With this approach, it was able to charge prices that were significantly higher than what it had initially estimated.

There are two main lessons we can learn from this marketing agency's experience. First, even for the same product or service, the range of reasonable prices can differ dramatically for different customer segments. This is particularly the case in many business markets. Second, the company must conduct careful competitor analysis at the outset, and then periodically, to understand competitors' prices and what prices customers consider as reasonable. Without these insights, the digital marketing agency would have needlessly underpriced its services and perhaps even inadvertently started a price war with competitors.

How to Measure the Customer's Range of Reasonable Prices

One way to find the customer's range of reasonable prices is by trial and error. The company can keep raising its prices periodically until suddenly, it sees a sharp drop-off in sales. At this point, the price has passed the high end of customers' range of reasonable prices. On the other hand, if the company keeps lowering its prices, sales will take off when they stray too low, beyond the reasonable range into the "screaming deal" range. Alternatively, and counter-intuitively, sales could drop off significantly as well at these low price levels, if customers become suspicious of the product's quality.

To understand why this is the case, marketing professors Jagmohan Raju and Z. John Zhang describe the cautionary experience of a Chinese manufacturer of exquisite silk scarves who enthusiastically set prices of 200-300 yuan for its scarves. Its main competitor, a premium French brand (and you can probably guess which one) sold the same scarves for ten times as much money. The scarves were identical because the Chinese company manufactured the French brand's scarves.

Even though the scarves' objective quality was identical and its price was one tenth of the competitor's price, the company still made no headway in sales. It turned out that Chinese consumers mainly buy silk scarves to give as gifts. Instead of attracting customers, the scarf's low price was a turnoff, because people wanted to impress their recipients by giving them something expensive. Selling such a high-quality product at such a low price repelled people instead of attracting them.

It is inadvisable to use this trial and error method of varying prices to discover the product's range of reasonable prices for two reasons. First, the method is fraught with risk, and the possibility of costly missteps. Second, a simpler, structured survey-based method can be used to do the same thing. To assess the customer's range of reasonable prices for a particular product, the company can use the following simple four-step procedure instead:

Step 1): Start with a clear definition of the product category that makes sense to the customer.

Marketing scholars call this a "goal-derived category[12]." Examples of such categories are "What to eat for lunch" for individual consumers and "Services to manage my company's digital marketing" for business customers.

Step 2): Ask the customer to divide the category into quality levels that they consider to have meaningful differences. The responses will typically contain 3-4 levels. This is what a customer may come up with for the category of "what to eat for lunch":

- When I want a quick bite to eat, and don't want to spend too much, e.g., food truck or vending machine.
- For daily lunch to eat at my desk, e.g., a carry-out sandwich.
- Occasionally when I want to take my full lunch hour and sit down and eat in a restaurant.

In a B2B context, for the digital marketing agency, customers in its medium-sized hospital segment fell into three categories based on their needs. They were those who wanted full service, those who wanted a limited set of services without any "bells-and-whistles" such as app development, and a third group who wanted only the essential services of email marketing and website management. With this information, the agency created three different solution bundles.

Step 3): For each quality level, ask customers the question, "What is the range of prices you consider to be reasonable and would be willing to pay?"

The digital agency called marketing executives in a dozen of its potential customers and asked them about the pricing schedules they had received from competitors. While a few were non-committal, most customers had little hesitation in sharing this information with the agency. As you can imagine, this was treasured information, which the agency obtained by just picking up the phone and asking clients.

Step 4): Use the values provided by the customer to establish the range of reasonable prices by quality level and create a graph. Figure 6.1 provides one example of such a graph. It shows that the customer considers $1-2 to be a reasonable price range for a taco or hot dog from a food truck, $4-6 for a carry-out sandwich, and $10-15 for a sit-down lunch.

With this systematic and relatively straightforward method, the company will be able to obtain the customer's range of reasonable prices and use this information as an input into making pricing decisions.

THE INFLUENCE OF PRICE CUES ON CUSTOMER PURCHASE DECISIONS

While the internal reference prices we have considered so far in this chapter are the ones customers know, external reference prices are encountered during the purchase decision process. As we saw earlier, customers' knowledge of specific prices is poor. Consequently, they are susceptible to influence by prices encountered during the shopping process and use them as reference points. Marketing experts think of external reference prices as "price cues" that can be utilized by the company to create an illusion of customer value[13].

Because the marketer typically supplies external reference prices, they provide a real opportunity to influence customers' judgment of prices. What is more, marketers have considerable leeway in providing reference prices to customers. They can use advertisements specifically to highlight a price or make a comparison with a competitor's price, they can generate reference prices through cleverly designed price tags, signs, or labels, and they can even use prices of adjacent items in the store or website to create influential external reference prices. Here are five of the most common and useful price cues that marketers use to influence the purchase decisions of their customers.

1) "WAS $X, IS $Y" PRICES (WHERE X > Y).

Among the most efficient ways to provide an external reference price to customers is to prominently display the original higher price and the mark-down side by side. For instance, Le Creuset's iron-handled cherry-colored skillet will be listed at $285 at Williams-Sonoma and Cutlery And More, but sold at $200, implying that the buyer is getting a deal[14]. Such supplied prices are also known as manufacturers' suggested retail prices. This method of providing an external price works for two reasons. First, the most obvious and logical reference price for any product is its previous price or its actual price, if it is on sale.

Saying that the product's current price is lower than its previous price or the normal price is to imply that the current price is a bargain. It is a logically compelling assertion that has persuasive appeal because the evidence is in front of the customer.

Second, combining a prominent higher reference price with either a "Sale" sign or a sign that generates urgency such as "While supplies last" or "For a limited time only" makes the reference price even more useful[15]. In one study, when sale signs were placed next to prices of dresses in a catalog without actually changing prices, sales jumped by 57% compared to a control condition with the same prices but no sale signs.

Despite its effectiveness, it is important to use this price cue sparingly for two reasons. First, academic research shows that if every item in the store is tagged in this way, the cue's effectiveness diminishes. The best outcome is obtained when less than half the items in the store, catalog, or brochure are tagged. A related, though less compelling price cue is to indicate that the displayed price is an everyday low price. While such labeling may burnish the store's price image by conveying stability and low prices, it is also likely to put a brake on customers' urgency to purchase. Second, the company should also take care to stay within ethical and legal restrictions on using supplied reference prices. Specifically, Code of Federal Regulations in the United States warns[16]:

> "Typically, a list price is a price at which articles are sold, if not everywhere, then at least in the principal retail outlets which do not conduct their business on a discount basis. It will not be deemed fictitious if it is the price at which substantial (that is, not

isolated or insignificant) sales are made in the advertiser's trade area (the area in which he does business). Conversely, if the list price is significantly in excess of the highest price at which substantial sales in the trade area are made, there is a clear and serious danger of the consumer being misled by an advertised reduction from this price."

The gist is that artificially inflating the displayed reference price before applying a seemingly large discount to it exposes the company to accusations of misleading customers and potential liability[17]. A common way to use this price cue is to vary prices, keeping them at the reference price level at some times, and lowering them to the sale price on other occasions, a method that is known as Hi-Lo pricing.

2) CHARM PRICES THAT END IN 9.

Marketers refer to prices that end in 9 (e.g., $3.99 and $199) as "charm prices." Many companies use charm prices to price all their products. In marketing, there is a long history of using them. The first known study on charm prices appeared in 1936[18]. Since then, dozens of studies have looked at the question of whether charm prices work. While the results are not always consistent, there is sufficient evidence to indicate that charm prices do encourage customers to make purchases. Across the research that finds positive effects of charm prices, the increase in customers' buying behavior is substantial—the lowest increase is around 5%, and the highest growth is over 75%[19]. Charm prices are particularly impactful for new and unfamiliar items. They are also influential when customers are unfamiliar with the product's regular price[20].

Charm prices influence customers in two distinct ways. First, they create the sense that the product's price is lower than it really is. Many people underestimate a charm price because when eye-balling it, they use what psychologists call a "truncation strategy[21]." They only pay attention to the leftmost digits of the price instead of all its digits. For example, a product priced at $7.99 (7-something) appears to be cheaper than the same item priced at $8.00 (8-something). Thanks to truncation, the charm price helps the product's sales.

The second reason is that when a company uses charm prices throughout a store, catalog or website, it creates a holistic low-price image for the retailer[22]. Once such an image is created, shoppers stop paying attention to actual prices or comparing them to competitors. They are convinced that the company's products will be cheap, and they purchase accordingly. This short-cut in customer decision making is the real strength of charm prices for the seller.

3) PRICES ENDING WITH AN EVEN NUMBER OR WITHOUT A DOLLAR SIGN PREFIX.

Because charm prices create the image of low price, economy, and thrift, they are shunned by companies who want to use price cues to create a different frame of reference for customers, one of exclusiveness and prestige. This is the reason why iconic Louis Vuitton bags have list prices that end in round numbers. Its Capucines bag is priced at $5,300, and the Montaigne is $4,200. This is also why Rolex watches are listed at $42,000 for the Oyster Perpetual Day-Date 40 Everose gold watch and $62,500 for the Platinum model[23]. These products simply would not have the same cachet if they were listed at $5,299 for a Louis Vuitton bag or $41,999.99 for a Rolex watch. Luxury brands, and the luxury retailers who sell these brands prefer to use prices that are whole round numbers.

The same logic of exclusiveness applies to presenting prices without a dollar sign prefix or writing out prices instead of using numbers (twenty-five dollars instead of $25) in a high-end spa, restaurant, or bar. In one study conducted at an upscale New York restaurant, lunch customers spent about $5.55 more when they received menus devoid of dollar signs compared to the regular menu. This translated to an 8% increase in customer spending[24]. However, the study's authors did sound a cautionary note that is worth noting. They said, "As much as we might like to believe that we can earn a quick buck by changing the type and presentation of [prices in] our menus, it is clear that larger operational factors have a much larger impact on purchase behavior than price typography does." Essentially, this and other price cues operate at the margin and have relatively small effects on customer behavior when compared to delivering a high-quality product or a memorable experience.

4) ADDING AN ARTIFICIALLY HIGH-PRICED ITEM IN THE PRODUCT LINE.

A few years ago, I worked with an entrepreneur (let's call her Hilda) who designed and sold jewelry through trunk shows in upscale boutique stores. At the time, Hilda was starting out and only had two items to sell: a $100 bracelet and a $400 jewelry set that included a more elegant bracelet, earrings, and a chain. (She had tried to sell the earrings and chain separately, but didn't have much success). The left panel of figure 6.3 illustrates this product line. From her pricing inputs, it was clear that the bracelet was by far the most expensive item to make. Consequently, Hilda made very little money by selling the bracelet alone. However, the $400 set was very profitable because the costs of making the earrings and chain were much lower.

Hilda had a unique problem. When she displayed the bracelet and the jewelry set at trunk shows, almost every customer purchased the bracelet, and hardly anyone bought the set. When asked why, her customers told her the set was too pricey. Hilda was considering lowering the set's $400 price tag substantially in response to this customer feedback. However, since the price is the most effective driver of profit, this would have meant devastating her profit as well.

Instead, she used one of the most reliable and effective price cues known to marketers today. She added a decoy or an artificially high-priced item to her product line. Some pricing experts call the decoy an anchor[25]. Specifically, Hilda designed a slightly more elaborate version of a jewelry set, studding the pieces with a few extra precious stones. Its price, however, was outrageously high, a whopping $2,500. The right panel of figure 6.3 illustrates Hilda's new product line. When the three options were displayed, the expensive set appeared to be a terrible value to everyone who saw it. However, because of this, it performed its job perfectly.

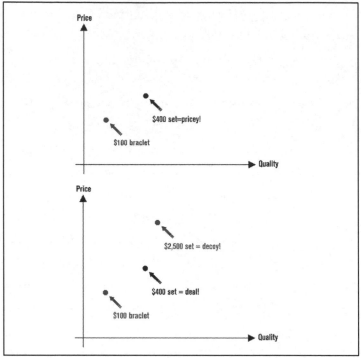

Figure 6.3 Decoys work by making the target option appear to be a great deal

It made the $400 set that Hilda wanted to sell seem to be a terrific value. Not surprisingly, once she introduced the decoy, sales of the $400 set jumped. In fact, in the trunk shows over the next two months, she sold more $400 sets than the $100 bracelets, an amazing turnaround.

Decoy options are now used in virtually every industry, from $100 hamburgers to Hublot's one million dollar Black Caviar watch, from prominent but unaffordably priced enterprise "all-in" software to fully-loaded farm equipment that may cost three or four times as much as the base model of the machine. If your company does not use decoys strategically to promote sales of highly profitable products in your product line, it should do so.

Decoys are a straightforward and inexpensive price cue to increase sales of high-margin products.

5) PRICES OF UNRELATED PRODUCTS DISPLAYED NEXT TO THE COMPANY'S PRODUCT.

A few years ago, I conducted a study with Professor Itamar Simonson of Stanford University to study how adjacent prices affect customer behaviors[26]. We sold sets of three music CDs on eBay where the middle CD had a starting bid price of $1.99, and the adjacent CDs were priced at either $.99 (low adjacent price) or $6.99 (high adjacent price). Adjacent prices had a huge effect on the middle CD's final price. In the high adjacent price condition, eBay shoppers ended up bidding the $1.99 CD to an approximately 9% higher final price when compared to the low adjacent price condition.

Similarly, a team of consultants led by Rob Docters described an experiment conducted by Walmart in 2008 in which it sold Coke bottles either in the traditional beverage aisle or the sportswear aisle and found that it was able to charge a much higher price when Coke was displayed next to the higher priced sportswear[27]. These studies make an important and useful point for pricing. The influences of external prices do not have to come from the product's price; adjacent prices can also have an impact on customer purchases.

Adjacent prices serve as important reference prices because many customers are inherently uncertain about the value of products they are considering for purchase. Such prices do not even have to be for the same product. Any encountered price, even that of an entirely unrelated product, can affect customer judgments. In a study conducted by consumer researchers Joe Nunes and Peter Boatwright[28], the authors sold popular music CDs next to sweatshirts that were alternately priced either at $10 or $80 (at half hour intervals) on a famous boardwalk. Beach-goers were willing to pay only $7.29 for the CDs when they were displayed next to $10 sweatshirts, but their willingness to pay jumped almost 18%, to $9, when the same sweatshirts were labeled with an $80 price tag. Even more impressive was the fact that most consumers did not realize that the prices of sweatshirts, or what the authors called as "incidental prices," were affecting their behavior. The results of this and other studies show that surrounding prices, even when they have little to do with the product, matter almost as much as the product's price. To you, the main takeaway is that to the extent that you have control where and how your product is displayed, you should be judicious in this selection, choosing to present your product next to other high-priced products.

In conclusion, according to the *value pricing framework*, the manager's task is not done after deciding what the product or service's price should be. They also need to work out a strategy to present and display these prices to customers in ways that influence their decisions favorably. Important to point out, none of the price cues we have discussed cost much money or take much time to implement. They have significant positive effects on customer behavior. Price cues are low hanging fruit that can be easily utilized by every company to increase its sales and profits.

CHAPTER SUMMARY

In this chapter, we saw that customers judge every price in relation to other prices. The customer's reference prices play two important roles in the *value pricing framework*. Their first role is informative, to provide you with an understanding of the range of prices that customers consider as reasonable for your product. If you keep your product's price within the range of reasonable prices, you can draw the attention of your customers away from price comparisons and price-based choice towards a consideration of non-price attributes that differentiate your product from others.

The second function of reference prices is informative. Whether it is "Was $X, Is $Y" labels with or without sale signs, charm prices that end in 9, round prices, leaving out the $ sign in pricing displays, adding an artificially high-priced item to a product line, or strategically influencing which incidental prices the customer is exposed to, price cues cost little money, can be implemented quickly, and have palpable impact on customer behavior. Price cues provide managers with a variety of tactical ammunition to impact the product's sales and profit at the point of purchase.

[7]

THE VALUE PROPOSITION

If you don't know where you are going, any road will get you there. - Lewis Carroll

Many managers think of pricing as a tactical instrument, similar to a rifle in an arsenal, or a wrench in a toolkit. When it is needed, take the tool out, use it, and then put it away. This tactical way of thinking about pricing is even ingrained in the popular Four Ps marketing framework that every marketer learns in Marketing 101. It tells marketers to "put the right product in the right place at the right price at the right time," implying that a price is specific to a particular context and is framed by a specific location and time.

When pricing is conceived of so commonly as a tactic, is it surprising that managers use it tactically? When a store needs a quick boost in sales, it runs a short-term sales promotion. When a car dealership strains to meet its quarterly sales quota, it gives discounts to customers who purchase a vehicle before the quarter ends. If a major competitor changes prices on a particular travel route, an airline follows suit, matching the competitor's prices. A software company offers a free trial or low introductory pricing to new customers, because "that is how it's done in our industry."

No doubt, some of these pricing moves are effective, leading to successful outcomes for the company. However, their weakness lies in the fact that they are reactive, isolated responses to a particular context, instead of being part of a concerted and thoughtfully-developed method that weights costs, customer value, and reference prices in a considered way every time.

The trouble with reactive pricing is evident when a manager's tactical objective (say, to meet the quarterly sales quota) collides with the company's value proposition (to create and maintain a premium brand image) and its long-term goals of having a strong brand, and a loyal, engaged customer base. The sale of each discounted product to meet the manager's quarterly sales quota creates a permanent blemish on the company's brand, leading to far more financial harm by irretrievably eroding brand equity[1]. Performed in isolation, tactical pricing actions may have short-term benefits but are just as likely to produce long-term, permanent damage to the company.

A more useful way to think of pricing decisions is to see them as grounded in the company's marketing strategy. In the *value pricing framework*, pricing decisions are based on, supported by, and contribute to delivering the company's core value proposition, rather than achieving its specific short-term tactical objectives. With this way of thinking, it makes little sense to make pricing decisions in isolation or on an ad hoc basis. Instead, even relatively common pricing activities such as limited-time price promotions and using price cues at the point of sale are designed and executed to implement the company's marketing strategy. The strategy articulates which customers are being targeted and for what purpose, who its main competitors are, and on what basis the company's product is differentiated from other offers in the marketplace. Strategic pricing decisions support well-articulated value propositions of the enterprise.

WHAT IS A VALUE PROPOSITION?

A value proposition captures the essence of a company's marketing strategy. In its most basic form, it is a succinct, formal expression of the company's marketing strategy, described in a customer-centric way. Instead of listing each of the company's capabilities, assets, resources, and priorities, a value proposition takes an "outside-in" view of the company. It describes the value of the company's product to the customer, seen from the customer's point of view. To understand this idea, let us look at some definitions provided by leading marketing experts in Table 7.1.

The definitions in Table 7.1 share two common characteristics. First, they describe the benefits that customers receive from the product, and second, many of them (but not all) explain how the company's product differs from its competitors. Let's develop each characteristic in detail, and then develop our own definition of value proposition that can be used for pricing decisions.

In the *value pricing framework*, the value proposition refers to the product, not the brand or the company, and describes the marketing strategy for the product. It answers two significant questions about the company's purpose in offering the product, the creation, communication and delivery of value to targeted customers, and its standing in relation to competitors' offers.

Authors	Definition
Philip Kotler and Kevin Lane Keller	The value proposition consists of the whole cluster of benefits the company promises to deliver. It is a statement about the experience customers will gain from the company's market offering and from their relationship with the supplier.
Noel Capon	The value proposition is the heart of positioning that provides a convincing answer to a deceptively simple question: Why should target customers prefer the firm's offer to competitors' offer?
Russell Winer and Ravi Dhar	A one-paragraph summary of a product or service's differentiation strategy and positioning to each target customer group; in short, a statement of why the customer should buy that product or service rather than the competitor's.
Alex Osterwalder, Yves Pigneur, Greg Bernarda and Alan Smith	A value proposition describes the benefits customers can expect from your products and services.
Ralf Drews & Melissa	Value proposition = Customer value X Uniqueness X Sustainability.
James Anderson, Nirmalya Kumar, and James Narus	A list of all the potential benefits target customers receive from a market offering. (All-benefits value proposition)
	All favorable points of difference a market offering has relative to the next best alternative. (Favorable points of difference value proposition)
	The one or two points of difference (and, perhaps, a point of parity) whose improvement will deliver the greatest value to the customer for the foreseeable future. (Resonating focus value proposition)

Table 7.1 Value proposition definitions presented by leading marketing experts[2]

1) WHAT BENEFITS WILL THE CUSTOMER RECEIVE FROM THE PRODUCT?

Relying on the customer's value grid that we developed in Chapter 5, the value proposition answers this question by describing specific product features and the benefits they deliver to the customer. The description of value delivery can take two forms. Some companies just generate and then use a list of all the product's features for marketing it. They provide this list to customers and let them figure out which features matter to them. Others go a step further and base their marketing programs on the benefits the customer derives from the product's features. This latter approach is advocated by the Kotler and Keller definition in Table 7.1.

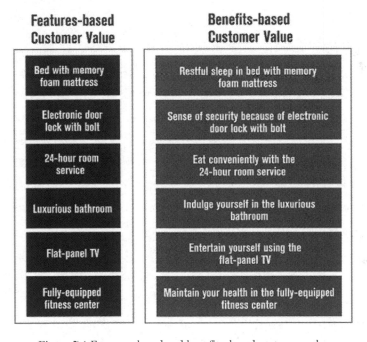

Figure 7.1 Features-based and benefits-based customer value

Returning to our hotel room example from Chapter 5, Figure 7.1 shows the two different ways of describing the hotel room's value to the customer, one using features (left panel) and the other using its benefits (the right panel) to the customer.

An enumeration of the product's features and benefits is a major component of every value proposition. However, the manager still needs to consider how the benefits compare to the alternatives available to the target customers. This comparison is of particular importance when making pricing decisions because as we have seen, customer evaluations are relative rather than absolute.

2) WHY SHOULD THE CUSTOMER BUY FROM THE COMPANY INSTEAD OF A COMPETITOR?

To explain the product's value to customers in a relative sense, by mirroring buying decisions, the value proposition also describes what is unique about the company's offer relative to its competitors, from the customer's point of view. According to marketing professors James Anderson, Nirmalya Kumar, and James Narus, the company's value proposition provides all the favorable points of difference that a market offering has relative to its next best alternative. To describe the product's uniqueness, not only is a closer examination of its features (and benefits) necessary, but the manager must also identify the relevant competitive products and compare the features. With this comparative approach, every product has four types of features:

a) **Points of parity** (common or shared features). These are the features that the product has in common with competitors. The company's product performs comparably, so it's hard to claim superiority or to charge a higher price. From the customer's perspective, the product's points of parity are often "hygiene" features. When the product possesses them, they go unnoticed and unappreciated. They are taken for granted. However, when they are missing or removed, all hell can break loose. Just consider how rarely, if ever, you have appreciated clean sheets when checking into a hotel room, but how revolted and enraged you would feel if you saw a prominent, funny-looking stain the next time you checked into a nice hotel. Clean sheets are a point of parity for nice hotel rooms.

b) **Points of superiority** (unique, superior features). The product clearly and verifiably outperforms on these features relative to competitors. They allow the company to claim superiority, and to differentiate its product, creating a branding and pricing advantage. Points of superiority can arise from different sources. They can be the result of technical innovation, patent ownership, a unique business model bringing together multiple competencies, or simply a longstanding feature that is associated with the product. For example, I recently stayed in a hotel where guests enjoyed a spectacular view from their rooms of a snow-fed lake with mountains in the backdrop. No amount of competitive posturing or effort could replicate this hotel's core point of superiority, namely its location, and the view. Points of superiority are prime candidates to differentiate the company's product from its competitors.

c) **Points of inferiority** (unique, inferior features). No product is superior to competitors' offers on every single feature. If a restaurant's food is tasty, chances are it is not as healthy as a competitor who emphasizes healthy choices[3]. The features where the product clearly and verifiably underperforms competition are called points of inferiority. The performance of these features (or the lack thereof) can become the company's Achilles Heel because customers who value these features will shun the product. The hotel with the incredible view did not offer room service. Even worse, it did not have an on-site restaurant either. Customers had to walk a long way if they wanted something to eat, putting it at a disadvantage. For every point of inferiority, the company will have to offer a price concession, while it figures out how to achieve parity.

d) Points of dispute (contested features). These product features are hidden, hard to evaluate, or otherwise ambiguous so as to be contentious. Neither the company, its competitors, nor its customers are confident about whose features perform the best, or even if there is any difference between them. No matter how hard they try, customers find claims about these features difficult to resolve. In business markets, customers often use points of disputes as negotiation ploys to talk down prices or to pit one competitor against another.

Understanding which product features fall into each of the four categories is a major step towards creating an effective value proposition and using it for pricing decisions.

HOW THE VALUE PROPOSITION INFLUENCES THE COMPANY'S MARKETING STRATEGY

To be successful, every company must develop and use carefully crafted and defined value propositions for its products. After understanding and sorting the product features into the four types, the next step is to determine which features matter to the targeted customers and how they will be used to construct a value proposition. The company will choose the most valued point of superiority, usually called "point of difference" or "POD" in the marketing and advertising worlds, and make it the focus of the company's offer.

In effect, the value proposition becomes, "You should buy my product because it has this point (or points) of difference." More formally, we can define the value proposition as *a focused and targeted explanation providing the main reason(s) why the customer should buy the company's product instead of a competitive offer.* The scenically-endowed hotel in our example would say, "You should stay here because you will get to enjoy this fantastic view from your room" with the subtext that no other hotel in the area will be able to match this vista. Notice that in choosing this value proposition, the hotel is deliberately downplaying its prices, amenities, quality of bedding, or any number of features it could use to distinguish itself. It has determined that its view is the most influential POD that its customers will care about.

The effectiveness of the company's value proposition depends on how much the targeted customers value the POD, and the extent to which they believe it to be unique to the company's product and absent from others. Table 7.1 summarizes these two qualities plus four others that contribute to the value proposition's effectiveness.

The value proposition is important because the process of crafting and articulating it clarifies the company's marketing strategy. It guides managerial thinking on consequential questions such as "Which customers should we target and serve?"; "What are our strengths and weaknesses relative to our competitors?"; "What is unique about our product offerings?" and "What should our pricing strategy be?"

Quality	Description
Differentiated	The value proposition must state how the company and its products are unique and distinct from competitors. Whole Foods positions itself as a healthy food store, by creating an entire, unique ecosystem of suppliers, standards, and product assortment. Its value proposition, to nourish and delight to its customers, allows it to charge a premium price.
Superior	Distinctiveness, by itself, is insufficient. The attributes on which the company's offer differs must be seen as clearly superior by target customers. By famously "reinventing the circus," Cirque du Soleil provides excellent entertainment. It combines aspects of theater, ballet, and opera with circus-like flourishes of clown acts and acrobatics[4]. Its tickets cost twice as much as a circus.
Relevant	The product's distinctive benefits should be meaningful to target customers. Electric bicycles offer a superior way of commuting on the congested roads of a city like Houston and solve the hassle of finding a parking space. Even with below-cost price offers, they have not been successful because they are alien to the automobile-centric lifestyle of the city's residents.
Quantifiable	The company should be able to convert its product's points of superiority (and inferiority) into monetary value. In business markets, documenting financial benefits achieved through cost savings or performance enhancements through specific business cases are the core part of the value pricing process at Siemens Healthineers[5].
Credentialed	The company's claims of superiority and distinctiveness gain validity and are more likely to be converted into successful pricing actions when they are supported by third-party assessments and customer reviews. Being rated as a Consumer Reports Top Pick gives Toyota Prius the cachet to hold back promotional pricing events, as would being the city's highest-rated restaurant on Yelp.
Sustainable	Value propositions are only useful if they apply and can be used for a significant period. Consider the integrated business model of Southwest Airlines which competitors have not been able to replicate in decades. Similarly, patents allow value propositions of many drugs such as Lipitor or Viagra to remain potent for years. In contrast, newly introduced features like a particular flavor of ketchup

or a flat-panel TV in a hotel room can be easily copied and are less effectual as value propositions.

Table 7.1 Six qualities of an effective value proposition

In business markets, the product's value proposition boils down to one of three basic types, all of which are intimately connected to the company's pricing decisions. They are: (1) increasing revenue by finding new customers or growing business from current customers, (2) reducing costs by improving efficiency, and (3) improving productivity[6]. These value propositions are only credible to the extent that they can be quantified, and evidence about the claims documented and provided to customers convincingly. Business value propositions are also difficult to sustain because the company has to keep raising the level of benefits provided by the product year after year. We will consider these issues in greater detail in Chapter 10.

In consumer industries, things are a little murkier. Value propositions do not necessarily have to be backed by quantifiable evidence, but they have to be supported by a set of consistent and coherent marketing programs that are experiential in nature. Consider the success of a luxury brand such as Cartier. The strength of its value proposition is derived from the imagery of experiences associated with the storied brand (e.g., "The emotions experienced from wearing a Cartier watch") and backed by its superior objective quality and performance.

Alternatively, consider the emphasis given to the customer experience delivery by Jet Blue. Its top management characterizes the company's value proposition as "We think of ourselves as a customer service company that happens to fly planes." To deliver this value proposition, the company has undertaken significant investments in technology and customer service over a decade, making the customer's flying experience its core point of superiority[7].

HOW THE VALUE PROPOSITION INFLUENCES THE COMPANY'S PRICING DECISIONS

In the *value pricing framework*, the value proposition is one of the four fundamental inputs into pricing decisions. It plays a critical role by providing the manager with the direction, constraints, and guidelines for making pricing decisions. It adds strategic heft to individual price actions and consistency across decisions. Instead of making each pricing decision haphazardly to serve whatever short-term objective is most salient at that moment, pricing decisions are now woven together by a common thread with the overarching purpose of delivering the chosen value proposition. Pricing done in this manner goes beyond simply considering tactical issues such as meeting a sales quota or matching a competitor's prices.

We saw in Chapter 5 that value and price go hand in hand. Customers cannot judge a product's value without considering its price, and vice versa. Whether stated explicitly in so many words or not, the success of every company's pricing strategy is dictated by the potency of its value proposition. The company's pricing strategy, in turn, drives its pricing decisions such as the price levels of its products and services, the range of prices charged, the frequency of price changes, the type and depth of incentives given to customers, and methods of price presentation.

Marketing Strategy	Cost Leadership	Premium Branding	Comparative Framing
Pricing input emphasized	Costs	Customer Value	Reference Prices
Value proposition	"We have the lowest prices."	"We have the best quality."	"We are better than our competitors."
Operational focus	• Keep costs low • Add new features cautiously • Focus on efficiency	• Drive innovation • Emphasize quality & brand image • Delight customers	• Monitor competitors carefully • Imitate features • Drive costs down
Pricing goal	Low-price image	Premium brand image	Superior value image
Pricing tactics	• Use loss leaders • Use charm (9-ending) prices • Use everyday low prices to support low price-image • Publicize small margins • Encourage price transparency	• Use rounded prices • Avoid frequent price promotions • Offer product bundles • Reduce visibility of prices • Reward customer loyalty and referrals	• Respond quickly to competitors' price changes • Use price comparison advertising • Match competitors' prices • Offer low price guarantee
Examples of companies	Aldi, Walmart, Southwest Airlines	Schlumberger, Panera Bread, Cartier	Hyundai, Taco Bell, Sprint

Table 7.2 Three value propositions and their influence on the company's pricing

When making pricing decisions, the value proposition's primary role is to calibrate the weights that are assigned to the other three inputs, costs, customer value, and reference prices. In many instances, all three inputs will be considered and used. However, value propositions, and the marketing strategy on which they are based can also emphasize one of the three inputs far more than the other two. These cases can be categorized into three types based on which one of these three pricing inputs is emphasized.

When a company builds its value proposition around the idea of providing the lowest prices, it is called the "cost leadership" marketing strategy. When customer value is given top billing, and the company differentiates itself on quality, it uses a "premium branding" strategy. Finally, it can use a "comparative framing" strategy to position itself squarely as superior to competitors and encourage customers to evaluate the differences explicitly. Let's consider each of the three value propositions and how they affect the company's operational focus, primary pricing goal, and pricing tactics in greater detail. A summary is provided in Table 7.2.

COST LEADERSHIP

When the company adopts a cost leadership marketing strategy, its value proposition is built around the claim that "We have the lowest prices." Not surprisingly, it emphasizes its costs over other inputs when making pricing decisions. We have already studied the case of Costco, which embraced cost leadership as its long-term strategy. Walmart, whose low-priced heritage is "as relevant today as it ever was[8]" and the German discount grocer, Aldi, are other examples of cost leaders. Aldi is among the largest and most profitable grocery store chains in the world with more than 10,000 stores in 18 countries. Its statement of its value proposition provides an excellent example of cost leadership[9]:

"Our unique business model enables us to provide the highest quality products at the lowest possible prices. This value stems from the numerous efficiencies and innovations we've instituted at every level of our operation. Our stores offer the customer over 1,400 of the most commonly purchased grocery and household products in the most common size—in a smaller, more manageable environment designed with sustainable, long-term savings in mind."

Aldi's form of austere service is entirely different from Costco's model. Its operations focus is designed to keep costs low by only offering service features that provide economic value to target customers who are very price-sensitive and to be maximally efficient in producing the service. In keeping with its value proposition of "the highest quality at the lowest prices," Aldi's customers must perform many of the tasks done by employees in other stores such as returning carts after shopping and packing grocery bags. Aldi has an in-house distribution system, a flat organizational structure, fixed hours of operation, a high proportion of private label brands, and multi-use packaging, all of which help the company to lower costs.

In its pitch to customers, the prices of Aldi's products take center-stage. Even without going to an Aldi store or seeing an Aldi newspaper advertisement, customers know its prices are going to be significantly lower than its competitors are. Its value proposition produces a simple, straightforward pricing strategy focused on costs, and its value delivery system seeks cost leadership in the grocery business.

As the case illustrates, the primary goal of a cost leader is to establish and maintain a low-price image. To achieve it, cost leaders routinely price their most popular and iconic products at extremely low levels. Recall Costco's inflation-proof hot dog and soda combo that is still sold at $1.50, unchanged since 1985. Cost leaders also tend to use charm prices and other price cues to convey and bolster their low-price image. Walmart is notorious for prices that end in 7, and Aldi liberally uses prices ending with 99 cents. Another common theme is that cost leaders widely publicize their small margins and encourage price transparency. A common way to do this is with an everyday low-price approach for most products and price promotions sparingly. With a cost leadership value proposition, the company often lags behind its peers in offering new, cutting-edge features because they are costly to provide, but adds to customer value by keeping prices significantly lower than the competition.

PREMIUM BRANDING

When a company adopts a premium branding strategy, its value proposition is built around offering the best quality. It pays less attention to maintaining low prices or justifying its prices to customers and focuses more on providing premium products, services, solutions, and experiences with greater amounts of benefits to customers who are willing to pay for them.

Schlumberger is the largest oilfield services company in the world, with 100,000 employees, and revenues of $27.8 billion in 2016. Like other business markets, managers in the oilfield industry have deep-seated concerns about commoditization[10]. Many companies in this space compete for contracts on price. Against this backdrop, here's how J. F. Poupeau, president of Schlumberger's drilling group characterized its value proposition:

> "The Schlumberger company value proposition is lowering the finding and development costs per barrel, and this is being done through three focus areas. First is improvement in drilling efficiency, which is reducing flat time and improving footage per day. Second is the positioning of the wellbore, well placement and the description of the reservoir. The third leg is wellbore assurance, which is all about delivering a wellbore into which you can run and install a completion on the first try. It is about the integrity of the wellbore and guaranteed access to the reservoir. Everything that we do in the group is targeting these three areas[11]."

Consider how different Schlumberger's value proposition is in its focus from Aldi's, and how it leads to an entirely different pricing approach. Instead of providing the lowest prices to customers, Schlumberger's value proposition emphasizes the processes by which customers will derive the greatest economic value from its services. The feasibility of low prices is entirely ignored or downplayed, while the drivers of superior quality—greater performance, reduced downtime of the oil well, and greater productivity are emphasized. The company's pricing strategy is clear. The customer will pay significantly higher prices for Schlumberger's services, but receive greater quality and reliability, having greater economic, political, and even regulatory benefits for drilling. These benefits, in turn, will translate into cost savings, that will yield a net economic benefit to the customer.

Another company that uses a premium branding strategy is the casual restaurant chain Panera Bread. It defines its value proposition using two points of superiority, "craveable wellness" and "elevated experience." The restaurant delivers craveable wellness with superior fresh-baked bread, and healthier soups, salads, and sandwiches than its competitors. Its marketing campaign centered on the tagline "Food as it should be" reinforces this point of difference. The second differentiator, elevated experience, is delivered through a cozy and inviting ambiance. Using this value proposition, Panera Bread had the highest customer loyalty in 2017 of all casual chains, and its stores averaged annual sales of $2.6 million, and a profit margin of 16.7%, far higher than its competitors[12].

Companies using premium branding are always adding innovative features to the product and taking out old ones. For instance, Panera was among the first restaurant chains to allow customers to order online or using mobile apps in 2013, and the first to "clean" its menu by removing artificial colors, sweeteners, flavors, and preservatives from its offerings[13].

Panera's prices are higher than competitors, but well within the target customers' range of reasonable prices, a reference price of around $5 for breakfast and around $10 for lunch. In all their marketing and communication programs, prices are deemphasized, and the healthfulness and quality of the food items and experience are given center stage. This quotation from the company's CEO clarifies the role of pricing[14]:

> "Panera does not define value the same way that other companies do. While other companies are heavily discounting to lure custom-

ers back, we believe the opportunity lies in offering a better "total experience" to our guests. So while the rest of the industry competes to offer the cheapest $3.99 salad, we will focus on delivering a $12.00 salad for $5.99 to $7.99. That is value the Panera way and it gets to the core of our value proposition."

COMPARATIVE FRAMING

When the company uses a comparative framing marketing strategy, it deliberately positions itself in opposition to one or more of its competitors. It bases its value proposition around the claim "Buy our product because it is better than our competitors." In its pricing decisions, the company gives prominence to the reference prices used by target customers, rather than to its costs or customer value. The comparative framing strategy is favored by new entrants into an established market and is therefore commonly used by startups. It is also preferred by relatively minor players in industry or those who have lost their mojo and are trying to regain it.

Telecommunication service provider Sprint is a typical comparative framing strategy adopter. It had a marginal market share in the cellular phone services market ranging between 12 and 17% for a number of years. Even its senior executives conceded their company was an underdog. In describing Sprint's pricing strategy, CEO Marcelo Claure said, "It is not about chopping prices, it's about being competitive...Why do we have to be so different than the other ones [competitors]? We're going to match the price of our competitors, and we're going to double the data...we think the best way to change an image is to be very clear about what you stand for. Today we stand for the best value in wireless. You're going to see that in our advertising[15]."

Companies using comparative framing are obsessed with their competitors. They spend a lot of effort in gathering competitive intelligence. Rather than trying some novel pricing approach or shaking things up, they set their prices strictly with reference to competitors, usually settling for a lower price. Then they aggressively advertise this fact using comparative advertising. For instance, Sprint has used price comparisons for years. In a recent iteration, it promised to at least halve the bills of its more established competitors' AT&T and Verizon's customers if they switched to Sprint. It also offered to pay early termination fees incurred by customers because of the switch.

Comparative framing users favor pricing tactics such as price matching and low price guarantees, which provide customers with the assurance that they will receive the best deals. This strategy is usually not the first choice or the best one for any company. It resorts to this strategy because it does not have an advantageous cost structure like Aldi or Southwest Airlines nor does it have superior quality like Schlumberger or Panera Bread. With no clear point of superiority and with a marketplace position that is overshadowed by bigger, more powerful, and better-known competitors, it is forced to compete on price. When one or more companies in an industry base their pricing on the comparative framing strategy and are aggressive about maintaining lower prices, price wars can flare up[16].

As we have seen throughout this chapter, value propositions can and should be instrumental in guiding the company's pricing strategy. We will conclude this chapter by considering the case study of a startup called Know Your Company, which has used a unique value proposition and pricing strategy to carve out a successful business model. This case study brings together the key learnings from this chapter, showing how effective pricing and successful strategic positioning and execution go hand in hand.

HOW KNOW YOUR COMPANY USED AN UNCONVENTIONAL PRICING METHOD TO BUILD ITS BUSINESS

Know Your Company (KYC) is not a pithy admonishment to you, the reader. Instead, KYC is a startup with an innovative and simple pricing approach that goes against industry norms and enhances its product's value to customers. KYC makes a web-based app that is used by medium-sized businesses with less than 100 employees to strengthen employee relationships. The app encourages employees to share personal and professional information and provide candid feedback to supervisors[17].

Employees in large corporations perform these activities with in-house apps[18]. The KYC app provides the same benefits to smaller companies. It asks employees to respond to different questions several times a week. These questions request information ("What are you working on?"), solicit contributions ("Have you seen anything our competitors have done that's blown you away?") and encourage social interactions ("What are you doing this weekend?"). The responses are shared with everyone within the company, increasing procedural knowledge, building camaraderie and strengthening the corporate culture through regular communication.

Nowadays, web-based software is priced with a subscription model in which customers pay a site license fee and a per user fee on a monthly or annual basis. In the software industry, subscription pricing is preferred for at least three reasons. First, it reduces the customer's sticker shock. Paying $5 every month per employee seems a lot more reasonable than shelling out $100 upfront per employee. It also correlates with converting the software purchase into an operating expense instead of a capital expense, a far easier decision for the customer[19]. Second, subscription pricing capitalizes on customer inertia. Many customers continue to pay through automatic payment methods even after they have stopped using the product. Finally, subscription pricing results in a stable, recurring, and predictable stream of revenue.

Giving up these advantages and going against the conventional wisdom, KYC adopted a simple, front-loaded pricing structure. It charged its customers a one-time flat fee of $100 per employee, costing a typical customer with 30 employees $3,000. KYC chose this original pricing model for three reasons.

(1) **Sustained customer commitment.** Buying the software and paying for it, in the beginning, increased the business owner's commitment to using it and encouraging employees to use it on a regular basis and building a culture of communication. In KYC founder Claire Lew's words, "If you're truly invested in creating the best environment for your employees, you're getting feedback from your employees for life. Our pricing model encourages CEOs to start to see getting feedback in this way... As a result, CEOs put more energy behind Know Your Company when they roll it out. They talk it up to their employees, and they act on the feedback that comes from the software. Know Your Company becomes an initiative, a program—not just another web app

they're playing around with." Instead of capitalizing on customer inertia, the pricing method capitalizes on customer motivation.

(2) **Healthy cash flow.** Unlike subscription pricing where revenue is spread over time, with up-front pricing, the company books revenue right away. While this may make the income stream less predictable, it does hasten speed to reach profitability. KYC became profitable in its very first month of operation and remained profitable as it grew.

(3) **Company's success linked directly to customer's success.** The front-loaded pricing model is risky if the product does not deliver on its claims. If this happens, bad word of mouth can quickly turn away new customers because of the high commitment hurdle involved in purchasing the software. KYC has a strong incentive to keep delivering and satisfying its customers if it wants to grow.

With this pricing method, the product was very successful. In two and a half years after its launch, the small two-person company had amassed over 200 customers, generated over $700,000 in revenue, and $210,000 in profit. Interestingly, 70% of its growth came from existing customers adding new employees, indicating that as customers benefitted from using the software and grew in size, KYC profited in tandem. The following advice from Lew about pricing KYC's service aligns perfectly with the philosophy behind the *value pricing framework*:

> "What matters less is if the pricing model you've decided on is "popular" or not for your industry. Who cares if the way you price something or the way you sell something or the way you run your business is unconventional...What's most important is that you're

running a business on your own terms and providing real value to people by making some aspect of their lives better."

CHAPTER SUMMARY

In this chapter, we considered the role of the product's value proposition in making effective pricing decisions. Value propositions answer questions about the benefits customers will receive from the product and the reasons for preferring the company's product to those of competitors. The process of formulating a value proposition allows the company to understand which of its features are superior and inferior in performance to alternatives, and which ones are shared and contested. The company can then choose the key point(s) of difference, which it considers valued by its target customers and unique, relevant, quantifiable, and sustainable as the core of its value proposition.

The value proposition's primary role is to calibrate the weights given to the other three pricing decision inputs. While most companies are advised to balance between the decision inputs, individual strategies favor one input over the others. Depending on whether the enterprise embraces cost leadership, premium branding, or comparative framing as its value proposition, costs, customer value and reference prices will be given primacy by the company in its pricing decisions. In the *value pricing framework*, the value proposition provides the manager with the direction, constraints, and guidelines for pricing decisions. It adds strategic heft to pricing decisions and provides consistency across them. Rather than pricing haphazardly to serve whatever short-term objective is most salient at the moment, pricing decisions are now woven together with a common thread that has the overarching purpose of supporting and delivering the product's value proposition. Pricing conducted in this manner goes beyond idiosyncratic tactics such as covering costs or matching competitors' prices, and is synergistic, increasing the company's pricing effectiveness.

[8]

PRICE EXECUTION

There is many a slip 'tween the cup and the lip. – D. M. Moir

In the previous four chapters, we studied the role played by each of the four decision inputs in the company's pricing decisions. In this chapter, we will consider what happens after the pricing is done. In the *value pricing framework*, we make the fundamental distinction between pricing decisions and price execution to answer this question. Where pricing decisions involve either setting new prices or changing existing prices, price execution is about the individual and group processes of communication and coordination within the company, along with the interactions and negotiations with channel members and customers that culminate in the actual payment of the asked-for prices.

THE IMPORTANCE OF PRICE EXECUTION

The distinction between pricing decisions and price execution acknowledges one basic fact: *the prices listed in catalogs or web-*

sites or quoted to customers differ significantly from the prices that customers pay. We saw this discrepancy in the case of airplane manufacturers like Boeing and Airbus in Chapter 2. These companies have raised their catalog prices every year for the past several years. However, each time, they are talked down by customers. As a result, despite well-meaning and calculated price increases, actual prices earned by these companies have remained stagnant.

This gap between asked-for prices and realized prices, which is called the price realization gap in our framework, is found in every industry, although its size varies from company to company. Other terms commonly used by pricing experts to describe price execution include price action, price yield, "getting the price," and pocket price management.

The main reason for the price realization gap is that customers are given one or more incentives to close the deal and make the sale. Depending on the industry, these incentives can be substantial and take many different forms. What is more, many of these incentives are given concurrently which can lead the price realization gap to grow to a significant proportion of the asking price. In consumer markets, some examples of incentives given to customers include coupons, rebates, limited-time offers, buy one get one deals, flash sales, free or subsidized shipping, free installation, free warranty, sweepstakes, and loyalty rewards. In business markets, incentives can take the form of quantity discounts, cash discounts for prompt invoice payment, off-peak discounts to stock and sell products during the off-season, advertising allowances to run ad campaigns on behalf of the company, free or subsidized maintenance, warranties, education, or customization, slotting fees to rent shelf space in a retail store, and free or subsidized freight, in addition to lower prices that are negotiated during the sales process. In both consumer and business markets, the magnitude of incentives offered to customers can be significant. Here are a few examples to illustrate the scope of the price realization gap and highlight why it should be the focus of your attention.

- Incentives are routine in business markets. In many cases, they are so large they make listed prices seem irrelevant. McKinsey consultants Walter Baker and colleagues provide an example of the average amount of incentives offered by a linoleum manufacturer to flooring retail stores. They included at least seven different types such as a discount for ordering a certain quantity each time, paying invoices quickly, going past an annual volume threshold, an allowance for running cooperative advertising, and freight. Together, they totaled 25% of the listed price. The authors also provide other astonishing examples such as those of a furniture manufacturer with a price realization gap of 47% and an electrical controls supplier with a price realization gap of 72%.

- In consumer markets, virtually every company distributes coupons, and most consumers use them. In 2016 alone, 306 billion coupons were sent to American consumers. With the widespread adoption of digital coupons, redemption rates of coupons are starting to rise again after years of decline, indicating that coupons are increasingly important to customers in their buying decisions[1]. 85% of American consumers use coupons, and 42% of consumers claim to have saved more than $30 each week over listed prices of products by using coupons[2]. Given the average grocery bill of $77 per week[3], this is a substantial saving. Whether it is soup, toilet paper, or a pair of jeans, consumers who pay the product's actual listed price in a store or on a website are rare.

- In the restaurant industry, menu pricing experts Jack Miller and David Pavesic observe that "Discount promotions are now so frequently employed that regular menu prices are rarely charged... When sweepstakes, games, premium give-aways, and value meals are included (all of which are forms of discounting), an estimated 90 percent of all commercial restaurants will use some form of discounting[4]." So much for menu prices!

- While the rising cost of college education is a serious social issue[5], the truth is very few students attending private colleges pay the actually listed tuition fee[6]. Private colleges refer to the difference between the quoted tuition price, and what the student pays after grants, scholarships, and fellowships are factored in as the "discount rate." In 2005, the average discount rate at private colleges for all undergraduates was 34.3 percent. It has grown every single year since then, rising to 44.2 percent in 2016[7].

- When you fly in an airplane, the chances are that you paid a strikingly different price for your seat than the person sitting next to you. One 2014 tracking study found that prices for a New York–Miami flight changed 135 times and ranged between $197 and $474[8]. Another study found that on any given flight, price variation ranges between 2X and 8X for tickets. In other words, someone paying the highest price will have spent two to eight times as much as the person paying the lowest price[9].

With their diversity and scope, these examples make the important point that understanding and managing the price realization gap is a significant issue for most companies. At a minimum, you have to understand exactly how big the price realization gap is for your product, and why it is occurring. After that, if you find the difference to be problematic, you will need to put the appropriate procedures and controls in place to reduce and then manage its size. Both these things are crucial to the success of your company's pricing strategy. We will consider each of these issues in detail.

WHY DOES THE PRICE REALIZATION GAP OCCUR?

The price realization gap takes place in companies for different reasons. As we will see, when the reasons are diagnosed, some are significant red flags for the enterprise, while others are completely normal, or even indicative of positive signs for the future. It is neither possible nor desirable to reduce the price realization gap to zero. This would mean that every single one of your customers is paying every single dollar of your asking price. Such an event would only occur if: (a) you are the Soup Nazi[10], or (b) you have set your prices far lower than they should be.

First, let us consider the problematic reasons for a large price realization gap that are symptomatic of underlying business problems.

1) LACK OF COMMUNICATION WITHIN THE COMPANY

In most businesses, pricing decisions are made centrally, either as part of the periodic planning process or in response to changes in one or more of the decision inputs. However, prices are realized on the organization's frontlines by salespeople and store managers. This is because the transactions and negotiations with customers happen in customers' offices, in the store, or through email exchanges. In most companies, the people who make pricing decisions and those who are responsible for price execution are two different groups of employees.

Once pricing decisions are made centrally, the decided-upon prices, types and amounts of incentives must be communicated throughout the organization. Today, the internal communication is often accomplished using CRM or price optimization software. Also, the guidelines and instructions for giving incentives to customers along with details of the price offer authority (that is, who can provide the incentives) and guidelines (under what conditions the incentives can be given) need to be explained. This is difficult information to convey in a comprehensive and timely fashion, especially when the company changes prices frequently. In one B2B company I know, the salespeople do not have a clear idea of how stringent they have to be in following the rules for offering a quantity discount to customers. In the past, salespeople were reprimanded for offering undeserved discounts on some occasions, but not on others. In a few cases, they have been even congratulated by their manager for closing the deal. Such mixed messages do not augur well for future price execution.

Even more challenging is the communication of softer, and arguably, more relevant collateral information such as the company's underlying philosophy and strategic objectives from its pricing method, the role of prices in supporting the product's value proposition, and the rationale for the pricing structure and pricing levels. This information is most needed at the frontline where the employees interact with customers and have to provide explanations, answer questions, and deal with customer blowback. It is where the information is hardest to provide. One reason that the price realization gap occurs is that the procedural or the background information for the price change is not sufficiently conveyed from the center to the frontline. Relatedly, in many companies, there is a breakdown somewhere in the process so that those in charge of pricing decisions mistakenly believe that everyone on the frontline is on the same page with them.

Consultant Julie Meehan and her colleagues describe a case of a manufacturing company that spent a lot of money to revamp its pricing processes and calculate new list prices by accounting for their costs, customer value, and competitive dynamics. Essentially the company adopted and implemented the price-setting process advocated by the *value pricing framework*[11]. Yet, months after the new prices were rolled out, the product's profit had declined. When the company carefully investigated why, it turned out that the new prices were not communicated to the sales team nor were they given the rationale behind the prices. Without this understanding, there was a strong impetus to keep offering incentives to customers to close the deal. The elaborate decision-making process to determine prices was virtually useless because of the poor communication about the new prices that followed.

2) DIFFICULTIES WITH MEASURING AND TRACKING INCENTIVES AT THE
CUSTOMER LEVEL

A second reason has to do with simply not knowing what the
price realization gap is, either at the customer level, or even in
the aggregate, for the product, and how many and what amounts
of incentives customers are getting. Many companies do not
measure costs and allocate them to individual customer relationships. Instead, they manage and track costs at the level of the activity or the business function. For example, consider an
automotive manufacturer such as BMW, Ford, or Volkswagen.
As part of their relationships with car dealers, these companies
allocate a certain amount of money each year to allow each dealer
to run local television, radio, and print advertising campaigns.
This money is given as an incentive to the dealer who can spend
the money on advertising, or pool the money with other dealers
within a local market, add some of their own funds, and produce
these ad campaigns.

Depending on the industry, the incentive has different names
such as cooperative advertising, local advertising, cost sharing,
and market development advertising. Whatever the name, where
the car manufacturer is concerned, these expenses constitute incentives that are uniquely offered to each of its dealers. They
lower the actual price earned per vehicle from the dealer. Even
though these funds are allocated on a negotiated basis, many
companies collect and report this expense within their overall
advertising and promotions costs. This is just one example of how
information about individual incentives gets lost in the record-
keeping. Now consider all the other incentives offered to individual customers that are reported in the aggregate, and the scope

of the missing information is significant. The lack of visibility about what incentives each customer is receiving makes it very difficult to understand what price each customer is paying for the company's product.

The same logic applies to consumer markets. For instance, a Starbucks customer may redeem rewards stars for a free drink after purchasing products with different margins, and by availing of various rewards promotions. Because of the complexity of earning and redeeming rewards from various promotions[12], plus the use of other incentives such as free shipping, limited time sales, and so on, it is hard to determine what price the customer paid for the purchased products. Without an understanding of the prices customers have paid in the past, and the margin the company has earned, consider how challenging it is for frontline employees to prepare for and negotiate prices effectively.

3) PROBLEMS WITH CUSTOMER REACTIONS, ENFORCEMENT, AND COMPLIANCE OF OFFERED CONCESSIONS

When customers are given an incentive for the first time, they see it as novel and something of significant value. However, over time, customers become used to the incentive and start considering it as the status quo, and as part of the product offer. It becomes an entitlement. Taking it away, even when it is undeserved, produces customer outrage, and can result in the severance of the customer's relationship with the company.

Consider Starbucks' customer rewards program that is offered as a perquisite to loyal customers. Until 2014, the coffee retailer offered its customers one star for every purchase. When the customer had accumulated 12 stars, they could be redeemed for a free drink or food item. In theory, savvy shoppers could buy twelve tall coffees costing $1 apiece, and then redeem the 12 stars, accumulated at an aggregate expense of $12 (plus tax) for a $5 fancy venti drink, in effect earning a reward of over 40%.

In April 2016, Starbucks revamped this overly generous rewards program, making the rewards contingent on the amount spent rather than the number of purchases. Under the new program, customers had to spend $62.50 to earn a free drink[13]. From a pricing perspective, this was a smart move, entirely in line with the *value pricing framework*. However, many Starbucks customers were livid[14]. They were so used to taking advantage of the program, that they were understandably miffed they would not be getting 40% or 50% off the list price anymore. All this despite the fact that these rewards were a bonus, given in addition to the value of the company's products. The customers had gotten used to the incentives.

The same thing happens in business markets. A customer will be given a quantity discount first because they purchased more than the stipulated amount that year. However, from then on, they will come to see this discount as the status quo, whether it is merited by the amount purchased or not. Now replicate this scenario for every other incentive received by each customer and we can quickly see how challenging it is to enforce the rules.

WHEN THE PRICE REALIZATION GAP IS A GOOD THING

In certain exceptional cases, the price realization gap is a core aspect of the company's value proposition to its customers. The fact that such a gap between listed prices and what customers pay exists is communicated explicitly to customers and is used strategically by the company. The company implicitly promises its target customers, "When you shop in our stores, you will experience the thrill of hunting for and finding merchandise at an amazing bargain." The excitement generated from such a shopping experience is the primary hedonic value derived by customers, more so even than the actual products purchased. It is this experiential bargain-hunting aspect of the shopping experience that keeps customers coming back. In such cases, posted prices mean little and are used as signifiers to create a mostly meaningless external reference price against which customers calculate the bargain's size and evaluate whether the sale price is sufficiently discounted.

The poster child of this strategy is JC Penney, which grew to a multi-billion dollar business with millions of loyal customers by using this value proposition. Consumer psychologists Amitav Chakravarti and Manoj Thomas call Penney's pricing strategy a "bargain hunt" pricing strategy. In 2011, for example, the company ran close to 600 major sales promotions and sold three-quarters of its products at discounts of 50% or greater. In contrast, less than 1% of its products were sold at full price[15]. On paper, its price realization gap would appear to be spectacularly high, but on closer inspection, it is based on artificially posted prices.

For JC Penney, and other companies that have adopted the bargain hunt value proposition, trying to reduce the price realization gap, or switching to a more conventional value proposition can turn out to be disastrous. When the company tried to change its pricing to a "Fair and Square" strategy in 2012 by introducing lower everyday fixed prices and cutting down the number of promotions drastically, its sales fell off a precipice. Annual sales dropped by 25%, amounting to \$4.3 billion in lost revenue[16]. Customers defected in droves. The comments of one Penney customer from Florida summarized customer sentiment: "I come home and I cry over it, and my husband's looking at me, like, 'What's wrong?' I said, 'Penney's doesn't have sales anymore. I need my store back![17]'" Eventually, the company fired its CEO and reverted to offering deep discounts off dubious list prices, because that is what its core customers wanted and expected from the enterprise. In JC Penney's case, a large price realization gap was a key to building and maintaining a satisfied customer base that came for the thrills of bargain hunting, even when those bargains were illusions.

As the JC Penney case illustrates, when the price realization gap is created, monitored, and managed for strategic reasons such as to generate the excitement of "winning" a bargain, by providing a high reference price to customers to influence their evaluation of the product, it can be a strength, and contribute to positive outcomes.

In addition to the gap's size, the variation in the price realization gap also conveys useful information. If the company finds that the price realization gap is higher in a certain market, or with a particular customer segment, for instance, this may be an indication that its products are less valuable to these groups. It must then decide whether to withdraw from those markets or segments or figure out ways to increase the value delivered to them. Variation in the price realization gap could also arise from differences in the performance of individual salespeople, or in the strength of competitors in different markets. Whatever the reason, understanding these variations will provide useful insights to the manager.

CLOSING THE PRICE REALIZATION GAP

Once the size and the determinants of the price realization gap are understood, the company must take steps to reduce it. The solutions parallel the sources of the problem. The company must improve communication about prices within, and between its functional areas, different incentives given to each customer should be measured, tracked and monitored systematically, and contracts and agreements must be enforced so that incentives are only given when the customer has earned them. Let us consider these strategies for closing the price realization gap in more detail.

IMPROVING PRICING OPERATIONS

Pricing consultants Manmohan Sodhi and Navdeep Sodhi suggest a useful operations-focused method to reduce the price realization gap[18]. It is based on the Six Sigma process improvement methodology that is widely used in quality management projects. According to these authors, every gap between the list or quoted price and the realized price constitutes a "defect" because it hurts the company's financial performance. Pricing defects are caused by poorly designed or inadequate processes of communication, negotiation, monitoring, and control. Consequently, the authors suggest that improving price realization and closing the gap is a matter of improving current processes, and adding new ones if warranted to increase discipline in communicating and executing prices. They suggest the following five-step process, closely mirroring the Six Sigma methodology, to reduce the price realization gap:

STEP 1: IDENTIFY THE PRICING DEFECT

Sodhi and Sodhi suggest starting by defining the defect in the pricing process precisely, both in terms of its scope and its extent. We have already discussed a number of pricing defects earlier in the chapter. For instance, if a company finds that different customers are paying significantly different prices without any apparent rationale for these differences, this is a pricing defect. If the salespeople are clueless about the company's pricing philosophy or the repercussions that will come from giving away unwarranted discounts, this is a pricing defect. If customers are getting incentives without deserving them, this is a pricing defect. The three sources of the price realization gap described earlier produce a variety of pricing defects.

STEP 2: INVESTIGATE AND UNDERSTAND DETAILS UNDERLYING THE PRICING DEFECT

In the second stage, the company gathers data to know exactly how its current pricing process works. The goal is to build a map detailing the process by which pricing decisions are communicated, enforced, and controlled by the organization, up to and including the customer. The questions answered in this step include, "What chain of communication does information about a price change pass through?"; "Who has the authority to offer discounts to a particular customer?"; "Does the authority vary by size of contract or discount?"; "What is the verification and approval process, if any, to offer discounts?" and "How much autonomy does the salesperson have during the negotiation process on offering concessions?"

In my experience, depending on the questions posed, this can turn out to be the most challenging and time-consuming step of the process. One of my students completed a summer internship at a large oil-field services company. He spent the whole summer trying to understand and quantify all the incentives that were being given to different customer accounts. After ten weeks of full-time work, which involved digging through data housed in various divisions and functions within the company, he was able to gather the data he needed to understand the incentives being given to one major customer account. It is not surprising that many companies outsource this step to an experienced consulting company who will come in and do all the work.

STEP 3: ANALYZE THE DATA TO DIAGNOSE THE CAUSES OF THE PRICING DEFECT

Once the details have been gathered in step 2, the data must be analyzed to develop a better understanding of the pricing defect's significance, and how its size and occurrence are affected by various internal and external factors. The goal of this step is to identify the most significant causes of the defect. It requires both quantitative (to understand the defect's size with respect to its impact on measures of pricing performance) and qualitative (the organization's cultural and political milieu, the role and tacit influence of individual managers, etc.) factors to be considered in an unbiased way.

STEP 4: CHALK OUT A PLAN TO ADDRESS THE DEFECT BY IMPROVING RELEVANT PROCESSES

In this step, the company considers how to address the fundamental causes of the pricing defect, and the results that will occur from doing so. Some changes may be relatively straightfor-straightforward such as making sure that frontline employees have the necessary pricing information, or conducting regular company-wide sessions where senior executives explain the pricing philosophy and the company's goals from pricing performance, which we will cover in depth in the next chapter.

However, other causes identified in step 3 can be extremely pernicious, requiring a long-term plan of redressal. For instance, the Sodhis describe the case of a company in which there was a longstanding adversarial relationship between the pricing department and the salesforce[19]. The pricing department viewed the salesforce as incompetent and arrogant, while the salespeople saw the pricing managers as obstacles in their path to earning high commissions. As a result, they simply ignored or circumvented pricing directives, gave away incentives galore, and didn't care about price execution. When such a cause is identified correctly, it is still tough to solve the problem.

STEP 5: ESTABLISH METHODS TO TRACK, MONITOR AND MAKE ADJUSTMENTS TO THE IMPROVED PRICING PROCESS

Like most complex business problems, improving price execution requires time, sustained effort, and the commitment to continue the process once it has been undertaken. In this final step, the company establishes a set of checks and balances to ensure that all the employees involved in price execution, from the managers who make the pricing decisions to the frontline employees who execute them, and everyone in between, have adopted the changed process and are sticking to it. This is an area of pricing strategy where marketing takes a back seat, and expertise in operations leads the way.

SUMMARY OF THE OPERATIONS-FOCUSED APPROACH TO IMPROVING PRICE EXECUTION

The Sodhis' Six Sigma-based approach provides a structured way to think about how you can improve price execution in your company. It addresses issues of communication, measurement, tracking, enforcement and compliance with a single, integrated five-step process. This method's greatest strength lies in making you think more holistically about pricing questions, beyond the decision itself to more broadly about everything that has to happen within your company to realize the decided-upon price effectively. On the downside, many moving parts to this method contribute to its difficulty and lower the chance of successful competition. Taking up smaller and less ambitious projects first such as communicating the rationale for pricing in a general way to everyone within your company, making headway with them, and then moving on to company-wide, large-scale projects such as changes to the corporate culture is a good way to implement this method.

In the final section of this chapter, we will consider the key issue of pricing autonomy. The issue at hand is who within the company should be responsible for determining the final price offered to customers?

WHO SHOULD DECIDE THE FINAL ASKING PRICE?

Companies in business markets face this question frequently. When considering which incentives to offer, and then quoting customers the final asking price, B2B companies use one of two approaches. The first method is a centralized pricing approach where every price reduction from the list price or incentive that is offered to customers must be vetted and approved first by the sales manager or someone in the company's corporate headquarters. Naturally, this method grants little autonomy to frontline salespeople. The second, diametrically opposite way, is to use a discretionary pricing approach. This approach gives salespeople considerable discretion to negotiate prices and settle on the final asking price without intervention by the central office.

There are distinct advantages and disadvantages to both methods. When final asking price decisions are centralized, the company can use information from across the enterprise (for instance, customer feedback from other regions or painstakingly conducted competitor analysis). It also has access to sophisticated tools such as price optimization software, statistical modeling and analysis, and can apply the tenets of the *value pricing framework* to calculate the best final asking price for the customer. This is particularly useful when price quotes are being developed for custom projects. One manufacturing company that I know makes industrial brick kilns that are used for different applications such as pottery, glass-blowing, and pizza restaurants. Each kiln it makes is custom-designed and manufactured, and the manager has to do considerable work to calculate a reasonable price to quote potential customers. Frontline salespeople simply wouldn't be able to do this. Another benefit of centralized pricing is that it can prevent salespeople at the frontline from making impulsive or self-serving concessions that may bring home the sale, but hurt the company's bottom line.

On the other hand, field salespeople usually know idiosyncratic customer-specific information including data points that may be hard to quantify or analyze meaningfully on a centralized basis. While centralized decisions may miss it entirely, qualitative information from face-to-face encounters along with historical relationships with the customer allows the field salesperson to negotiate prices more efficiently when they are given the discretion to do so.

Which method, centralized or discretionary, leads to more successful pricing outcomes, both with respect to financial performance and with regard to positive customer and employee reactions for the company? A number of recent academic studies have tried to answer this question. In one study of auto-loan lending by car dealerships, the researchers found that when the lender gave each dealership's finance manager suggested interest rate guidelines for the loan based on the customer's creditworthiness along with discretion to negotiate, the managers were able to increase the loan's profitability by an average of 8.9%[20]. Other research also supports the superiority of decentralized pricing authority and giving salespeople latitude to negotiate the final asking price.

A study of 181 German companies in the industrial machinery and electrical engineering industry found that when the company delegated pricing authority to salespeople, the business unit exhibited better performance as measured by its market share and revenue. The benefits of decentralized pricing were even greater when salespeople were knowledgeable about their customers and when market conditions were volatile with frequent introductions of new products, and changes in competitors' sales strategies and customer preferences[21]. A third study conducted with B2B companies in Germany found an inverted U-shaped relationship between decentralized pricing authority and the company's return on assets. According to the authors, giving salespeople a moderate degree of autonomy in pricing negotiations was the best thing for the enterprise[22].

GIVING INCENTIVES TO FRONTLINE EMPLOYEES

The findings from these academic studies make a critical practical point: You must give at least moderate autonomy to frontline salespeople to negotiate final prices with the customer. However, autonomy is only part of the journey towards effective price execution. Once they are given pricing authority, realizing a good price is also a matter of incentivizing salespeople to be stingy with customer discounts and make it, so it is in their best interests to do so.

Salespeople are reluctant when the company modifies their incentive structure from one based solely on revenues brought in by the salesperson to basing incentives on the profit generated from the sales. This is a dramatic change by any stretch of the imagination, because as we will see in the next chapter, revenue and profit can often conflict with each other, and one is gained at the other's expense. However, when the company presents this change in earning incentives as an opportunity to earn extra commissions, price realization can improve drastically.

Pricing consultant Hermann Simon recounts the case of a multinational industrial company that was giving its customers an average discount of 16% on its listed prices[23]. This, by the way, is a relatively typical value in business markets, where price realization gaps can easily reach 50%. To reduce this so-called "money left on the table," the company instituted an "anti-discount incentive" for its salespeople. Mostly when the rep negotiated and achieved a sale with reduced discounts to the customer and realized a higher price, they received part of the additional revenue from the deal as commission. Once salespeople were rewarded for being stingy with discounts, it had an immediate effect on their behavior. Within three months, the average discount rate given to customers shrank from 16% to 14% without loss in sales, having the same effect as raising prices by 2%. As this discussion suggests, the key to effective price execution lies in providing autonomy to frontline employees and then giving them the appropriate incentives to negotiate in the interest of achieving a balance between sales and profit, instead of focusing on sales alone.

CHAPTER SUMMARY

In this chapter, we considered the importance of price execution, defined as the individual and group processes of communication and coordination within the company, along with the interactions and negotiations with channel members and customers that culminate in the actual payment of the asked-for prices. Most companies face a significant gap between asked-for prices and realized prices, which is called the price realization gap. The main reason for this gap is that customers are given one or more incentives to close the deal and make the sale. Depending on the industry, these incentives can be substantial and take many different forms.

We also considered three reasons for occurrence of the price realization gap: (1) the lack of communication within the company about the guidelines and instructions for offering incentives to customers, details of the price offer authority, offer guidelines, and the company's underlying philosophy and strategic objectives from its pricing method; (2) difficulties with measuring and tracking incentives at the customer level, specifically not knowing how many and what amounts of incentives customers are receiving; and (3) problems with customer pushback, and the enforcement and compliance of offered concessions.

However, we also saw that when the price realization gap is created, monitored, and managed for strategic reasons such as to generate the excitement of getting a bargain or to provide a high reference price to customers to influence their evaluation of the product, it can have a positive effect on outcomes. We also considered the Sodhis' five-step method of improving pricing operations, based on the Six Sigma methodology to reduce the price realization gap. The method relies on identifying, fixing, and then monitoring pricing defects. In the final part of the chapter, we compared the centralized and discretionary pricing procedure in business markets. The results of academic research show that the key to effective price execution lies in providing autonomy to frontline salespeople and then giving them the appropriate incentives to negotiate in the interest of achieving a balance between sales and profit, instead of focusing on sales alone.

[9]

MEASURES OF PRICING SUCCESS

In the state of nature, profit is the measure of right. – Thomas
Hobbes

The most common pricing decision that companies make
is a temporary price cut[1]. A specialty chemicals manufacturer may offer a discount on one of its product lines
until the end of the year. A medical devices maker may sell its
defibrillators for 20% off until its inventory runs out. A grocery
store may put organic bananas on sale for 29 cents per pound for
a week, marking it down from the regular 49 cents price. In all
these cases, the company's primary purpose is to increase the
product's sales, even when it has secondary reasons such as flush-
ing out its inventory or attracting new customers. The price cut's
effectiveness will be judged by how much the product's sales and
market share increase.

The Importance of Balancing Measures of Pricing Success

While such a laser-like focus provides a clear indicator of pricing performance and serves as a valid goal for managers, using sales alone to evaluate a pricing decision has significant downsides. In volume terms, the specialty chemicals company may sell twice as much of the discounted chemical as it did last year, but earn a significantly lower profit margin, and suffer a hit on its total profit. By cutting the price of defibrillators, the medical devices maker may increase its revenue and flush out inventory, but will simultaneously make customers wary of paying full price for its products in the future. Moreover, when they are sold at 29 cents a pound, customers will adjust their range of reasonable prices for organic bananas lower, making it difficult to go back to charging 49 cents.

Although it is an improvement, even considering the profit impact of pricing decisions is not enough. Every pricing decision that a company makes not only affects the company's financial performance as measured by its revenue and profit, but it also influences the perceptions of customers and employees. Some pricing decisions are seen as fair and transparent. They result in positive evaluations and strengthen relationships. However, others cause alienation and confusion. In the *value pricing framework*, we evaluate the success of pricing decisions by using four outcome measures.

In this chapter, we will consider how pricing affects each of the four outcomes in detail: sales (measured by revenue earned or units sold), profit (measured by profit amount, percentage increase in profit, or gross profit margin), customer satisfaction, and employee satisfaction, reflecting the reaction of customers and employees to the company's pricing policies and decisions, respectively.

The central theme of this chapter is that you should explicitly consider and balance the effects of your pricing decisions on all four measures instead of trying to maximize one. There is a tendency among managers only to emphasize sales, or at best, to pay attention to effects of price changes on sales and profit. It is the rare company that considers what its customers and employees think about its pricing strategy, and how they react to its pricing decisions. These latter factors can have certain effects on the success of pricing.

Because trying to maximize one of these four measures can affect the other three adversely, you should avoid trying to maximize just one or even two of the factors. Instead, your goal should be to make pricing decisions that "satisfice," that is, perform adequately on all four outcomes[2]. For example, to ensure that your customers are on board, and consider your prices to be fair and transparent, you may have to settle for a lower profit margin. Moreover, to empower your frontline employees, you may have to encourage them to decline sales to price-conscious customers who are not willing to pay the asking price[3]. Let's consider each of these four outcomes in greater detail.

USING SALES TO EVALUATE PRICING DECISIONS

The company's sales (or more accurately, its change in sales) is the most commonly watched and tracked financial measure to gauge whether a pricing decision is working effectively. In many organizations, it is the only measure used for this purpose. There are at least three reasons for this single-minded focus on sales.

REASON #1: THE IDEA THAT SALES GROWTH IS THE MOST IMPORTANT MEASURE OF THE COMPANY'S SUCCESS IS INGRAINED IN MANAGERS' THINKING.

For the past fifty years or more, business schools have taught and reinforced the notion that the firm's sales growth is hitched to its longer-term success[4]. Even today, if you read an article in the Wall Street Journal or tune into CNBC during earnings season, the first metric reported and weighted most heavily is how much the company's revenue grew that quarter or that year.

This importance given to sales growth for tracking the company's performance is based on the three-fold logic that: (a) sales growth shows that the company is able to attract new customers and retain existing ones, and a larger number of customers find its products to be of value; (b) as sales grow, the company will enjoy market power, and economies of scale in manufacturing, distribution, and marketing, leading, in turn, to its being able to compete effectively and earn higher profit margins; and (c) investors love companies that are growing quickly, and will run up their stock prices. Because of these three reasons, executives in established businesses and startup founders alike, are judged and rewarded or punished based on how quickly they can grow their company's sales.

REASON #2: WHEN COMPARED TO OTHER CUSTOMER-CENTRIC
MEASURES SUCH AS BRAND ATTACHMENT OR LOYALTY, THE MANAGER
CAN INFLUENCE SALES RELATIVELY QUICKLY.

In simple terms, all that is needed to increase sales is to lower the price. The only question is by how much. As we have seen in earlier chapters when we examined the roles played by customer value and reference prices, in both business and consumer markets, customers use price as an important consideration when making buying decisions. When the product's price changes, it has a quick and significant effect on customers' purchasing decisions. This, in turn, translates into measurable effects on the company's sales, whether they are defined by revenue or by units sold. The product's price and sales work as the opposite sides of a seesaw. When one goes up, the other goes down, as illustrated in figure 9.1.

For many managers, the quickest and the surest way to increase sales and to get rewarded for good performance is to cut prices. Because of this fundamental inverse relationship between price and sales, an increase in sales is considered as the most appropriate way to measure whether a price cut has worked. On the flip side, when companies raise prices, the one thing they are most afraid of is the adverse effect the price increase will have on their sales.

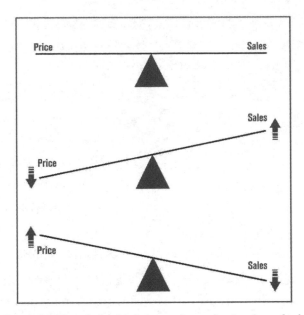

Figure 9.1 The relationship between the product's price and sales

REASON #3: IF A COMPANY KNOWS ITS PROFIT MARGIN, THE DESIRED OR
EXPECTED CHANGE IN SALES CAN BE USED TO SET A PRECISE GOAL FOR A
PRICE CHANGE TO BE EFFECTIVE.

Whenever a company makes a price change, the inverse relationship between price and sales allows the company to conduct
simple breakeven calculations to make two assessments:

(1) to precisely calculate how much sales change will be needed for the price change to be successful, and

(2) after the price change is implemented and the requisite period has elapsed, to retrospectively assess whether the price
change was successful or not, using the criterion of profit.

In both cases, pricing success is measured relative to the status quo, that is, relative to the product's sales before the pricing

change was made. Let's use a simple example to illustrate these calculations and their usefulness in evaluating a price change.

BREAKEVEN CALCULATIONS FOR A PRICE CHANGE AT THE SERVICE STATION

Consider a service station that performs oil changes on vehicles as part of routine maintenance. Let's assume this company uses markup pricing (covered in Chapter 4) to determine its price for the service. To change the vehicle's oil, the service station incurs variable costs of $20, and it uses a markup of 50% (which is its gross profit margin; gross profit margin = [price - variable costs]). Thus, the price for an oil change at the service station is $30. To bring in new customers and increase sales, the service station's business manager is considering whether to offer a 10% discount to all customers who purchase an oil change for the next one month. He wants to know whether running this price promotion is a good idea.

We can answer this question by reframing it as follows: **"With a 10% discount on the $30 oil change and a profit margin of 50%, what is the minimum sales volume increase that the service station will need to increase its profit from its current level?"**

This answer can be calculated using the following simple equation with only two variables, the price change, and the profit margin:

$$\text{Breakeven Sales Volume (\%)} = \frac{-(\% \text{ Price Change})}{\text{Margin} + (\% \text{ Price Change})}$$

Plugging in the service station's numbers, the breakeven sales volume for the 10% price cut is: - (-10%)/(50%+(-10%)) or .1/(.5 - .1), or 25%. In other words, if the service station offers a 10% discount on oil changes, it will have to perform 25% more oil changes than before the price cut to earn the same profit. Once this performance target is understood, the manager can go ahead and decide whether to run the promotion. After the one month is up, he can precisely determine whether the discount worked or not based on whether oil changes increased by more than 25% (the profit was greater than before, thus the discount worked) or less than 25% (the discount failed).

As this example illustrates, as long as you know the product's gross profit margin (the markup factor in the service station example), the "change in sales" metric offers both a clear target to aim for (before) and a yardstick (after) to assess the effectiveness of the price change.

The Limitations of Using Sales to Evaluate Pricing Decisions

Despite these benefits of using sales to measure pricing performance, relying on sales alone is problematic. The company's long-term success is dictated by multiple factors, not just growth in sales. The company must maintain a healthy profit margin, keep its customers satisfied with its pricing policies so that they make repeat purchases, and trust it, and hire and retain employees who are aligned with the company's culture, purpose, and ambitions. Each of these measures can conflict with the goal to grow the company's sales quickly.

1) SALES GROWTH AND PROFIT MARGIN ARE INVERSELY RELATED TO ONE
ANOTHER.

Let's conduct the following thought experiment. Imagine that
Tesla has just introduced a fully self-driving car for the American market. This new vehicle is a radical innovation, even when
compared to current Tesla models. It has no steering wheel, no
accelerator, and no brakes. All it has is two rows of passenger
seats facing each other. The car runs with voice commands, you
tell it where you want to go, and it will drive you there.

Who do you think is going to be the first to buy this fantastic
vehicle? If decades of research on adoption of innovations are any
guide[5], it will be the technology buffs, mostly middle-aged afflu-
ent male consumers, who will not care what they pay for this vehicle. Their greatest desire will be to be the first in their circle of
friends to drive this car (or actually to sit in it while it drives itself). In this early stage of market entry, Tesla's sales growth will
be steep, and its gross profit margin will be enormous. As it
grows its sales, however, and the vehicle becomes mainstream,
Tesla will have to start selling it to customers who are quite different from the price-oblivious technology enthusiasts. These
new buyers will be a lot more price conscious and a lot less enam-
ored of the vehicle's self-driving abilities. To make these incremental sales and to maintain sales growth, the company will have
to settle for a lower price and a lower profit margin.

What is true in Tesla's case in this thought experiment is also
true for every other organization. Not just for radical innovations, but for every product or service. This is a familiar pattern
for every product, not just radical innovations. When a company
starts selling a product, its early sales are made to customers who

value it, while latter sales are made to customers who value it much less and are therefore willing to pay less for it. This leads to a drop in the company's profit margin as its sales continue to increase. Sales growth and profit margin are inversely related. As one metric increments, the other one decreases.

What is worse, when a company emphasizes sales growth too much and uses it as the only yardstick to measure pricing performance, it tends to train its salesforce to offer price concessions too quickly, even if it means taking a hit on its brand equity or its profit margin. What produces a short-term benefit for the company (higher sales and sales growth) sets in motion the process leading to its longer-term demise. This occurs not only through lower profit margins but also through reduced brand equity and increased employee dissatisfaction[6]. Such a company does not care about other metrics that matter. All it wants to do is to grow quickly, without a clear understanding of the harm caused by its rapid growth.

2) THE CUSTOMER'S PRICE SENSITIVITY AFFECTS THE PRICE—SALES RELATIONSHIP.

Even though price and sales have an inverse relationship, they rarely move in opposite directions at the same rate as shown in Figure 9.1. In practice, the rate of change relative to each other depends on the price sensitivity of customers. When customers are extremely price sensitive (or price elastic, in economic terms), even a small price reduction can produce a dramatic increase in the company's sales (see top panel of Figure 9.2). On the other hand, when customers are not very sensitive to price and base their purchase decisions on non-price factors (that is when they are price inelastic), even large price changes will have minimal effects on sales (bottom panel of Figure 9.2).

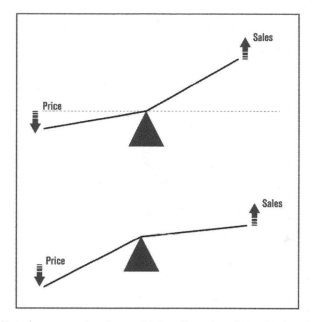

Figure 9.2 How the customer's price sensitivity affects the relationship between price and sales

When prices are increased, the effects on sales will reverse. Price sensitive customers will show significant buying decreases, but price insensitive customers will demonstrate little response. Thus, the change in sales will be a much stronger indicator of the pricing decision's effectiveness when customers are responsive to price changes. For insensitive customers, it does not matter. Pricing changes will not move the sales needle very much.

This nuanced relationship is just one case where the reactivity of sales to a pricing decision is affected by other factors, in this case, the customers' price sensitivity. Other factors such as excellent features, a rich (or recessionary) economic environment, and seasonal fluctuations can all influence the relationship between price and sales. The company must go beyond just using revenues or unit sales to considering other outcomes that have the ability to influence pricing success.

3) GIVING TOO MUCH WEIGHT TO SALES NUMBERS CAN BACKFIRE.

According to pricing consultants Hermann Simon, Frank Bilstein, and Frank Luby, when a company focuses too much on sales, it has adverse effects on its business strategy in two ways. First, always worrying about sales promotes what the authors call a "culture of aggression" within the company. Every pricing move is judged solely by its ability to keep market share or gain more of it, which in turn tends to promote pricing structures and decisions that erode profits and lead to bruising price wars with competitors.

The second adverse effect of a sales emphasis is to create a "culture of acquiescence" among the company's salesforce. They become anxious about missing a deal, and stop paying attention to price execution. Smart customers notice this anxiety and play hardball. Simon, Bilstein, and Luby explain the phenomenon in this way:

> "The ultimate sin in [such a] culture is to lose a customer and, thus, market share. In this case, companies essentially cede strategic control of their business to their customers, who gain the prices, terms, and conditions they want. Even when managers know that customers might be taking advantage of them in this manner, they feel reluctant or even powerless to change the situation."

This sounds like a dysfunctional environment to work in, doesn't it? It illustrates the importance of looking beyond sales and taking a broader view. Next, we will consider the role of profit in evaluating pricing effectiveness.

USING PROFIT TO EVALUATE PRICING DECISIONS

When a company goes beyond sales or market share and recognizes the importance of profit, it conducts its business differently. Instead of fostering toxic cultures of aggressiveness and acquiescence, it distinguishes between customers who derive more economic value from its products and those who derive less and is more open to raising its prices in ways that match the superior value received by some of its customers. Even when it offers incentives (not that there's anything wrong with that!), it is careful to structure them in ways that contribute to profit instead of eroding it. Moreover, it is careful to monitor incentive offers by ensuring that only customers who meet the stipulated criteria receive them. Each of these decision-making patterns is worth exploring in greater detail.

1) THE COMPANY IS RECEPTIVE TO PRICE INCREASES AND MONITORS INCENTIVES GIVEN TO CUSTOMERS CAREFULLY.

As we have seen, under a sales focus, B2B companies lean towards cutting prices and offer concessions indiscriminately to close the deal. B2C companies do not do much better. They keep increasing their acquisition costs per customer just so their customer base can keep growing, and use expensive measures to retain their current customers.

A couple of years ago, when I called my cable television provider to cancel the service, I was transferred to their customer retention department. I had been with the company for more than five years at that point, and the retention specialist was adamant the company wanted to keep my business. She kept offering me lower and lower prices, and I kept refusing. As a final offer, she offered me a permanent 20% discount, completely free service (worth more than $100 per month) for three months and a bundle of premium channels (worth around $40 per month) free for six months. At this point, I could not refuse the deal, so I stayed on. However, after the period of free service expired, I cut the cord anyway.

While the retention process benefitted me as a customer, I do not think it did the cable company much good. In the urgency to retain me, it stopped considering whether I valued it services to the same extent as I had done in the past. This sort of pricing lapse will be less likely to occur in a company that pays closer attention to its profit margins. It will be resistant to give away products or services and be much more open to raising prices when appropriate. It will minimize incentives, and make sure they are given only when customers deserve them. For instance, a quantity discount will only be applied to invoices where the customer has purchased the minimum required amount. When choosing between the alternatives of higher sales at a small or negative profit margin and fewer sales with a greater profit margin, such a company will choose the latter option.

2) THE COMPANY UNDERSTANDS WHICH CUSTOMERS DERIVE THE MOST ECONOMIC VALUE FROM ITS PRODUCTS.

One of the most potent and generalizable business truisms is that every customer derives different amounts of economic value from the same product. We have seen why this is the case in Chapter 5. Its implication for regulating the company's profit is that different customers will be willing to pay different amounts of money for the product based on differences in the derived value. The biggest challenge any company faces is to identify these high-value customers and make them a matching customized offer that is distinct from offers made to others. We will consider this challenge and how to address it in more detail in Chapter 10 for B2B companies and Chapter 11 for B2C companies. However, here, the key point is that acknowledging this crucial difference between your customers, and embracing the fact that your product might not be suited or appropriate for every customer goes a long way towards giving greater weight to profit in pricing decisions.

3) THE COMPANY USES EFFECTIVE PRICING TACTICS TO INCREASE PROFIT EARNED FROM CUSTOMERS.

Smart pricing strategy involves earning a higher profit margin from carefully selected and targeted customers. To do this, the company using the *value pricing framework* is astute about using a portfolio of effective pricing tactics. It prices the items in its product line carefully by offering choices to match customer valuation. One way to do this is with "good-better-best" priced options. Another is by providing price bundles that combine low-margin and high-margin products. We will study these methods in detail in Chapter 11. The company also uses consumer psychology to influence customers at the point of purchase by using price cues, which we discussed in Chapter 6.

The gist is that a company that adopts profit margin as a performance measure makes pricing decisions that are different, and more nuanced than one focusing only on sales and market share. The need to balance sales and profit equates to weighing the need to grow aggressively with the desire to be judicious and earn a profit from every incremental sale and customer relationship.

WHAT CUSTOMERS WANT FROM PRICING DECISIONS

Although most companies ignore this issue entirely, pricing decisions affect customers to a remarkable degree, in both how they respond, and the way they think of the company and its products. For instance, when a company raises prices, customers (obviously) do not like it. However, their reaction and the effect it has on the success and longevity of the price increase can vary significantly.

Take the case of Starbucks. In November 2016, the company raised prices of many of its products such as cold brews and baked goods by 10 to 30 cents apiece. It was Starbucks' second price increase within months[7]. Although a few customers complained and tweeted their displeasure, by and large, the price change was accepted without incident. Customers went on drinking their cold brewed lattes and eating their blueberry muffins. On the other hand, when Netflix raised its prices in May 2016 by $2 per month (a much smaller percent increase than Starbucks, mind you), all hell broke loose. Not only did Netflix's customers express their outrage at this price hike, but close to half a million of them canceled their subscriptions[8].

Why did customers of two popular, customer-oriented companies react in such dramatically different ways to price increases? The answer lies in how customers perceive the company's pricing decisions, particularly its price increases. Customers want three things from a company where its pricing policies are concerned: fairness, transparency, and stability. When price changes are fair, transparent and stable, customer reaction is positive at best and muted at worst. However, when one or more of these qualities is lacking, there is the potential for backlash. Let us consider each of these three characteristics in greater detail.

1) PRICE FAIRNESS

As we have seen throughout this book, prices are inextricably linked to the product's quality. For customers, prices concretize the sacrifice they will have to make in the exchange. Both the linkage of price with quality and the salience of financial sacrifice mean that customers are sensitive to understanding why the price is what it is. Is the company's price reasonable? Does the product's quality merit its asking price? Is the company keeping its promises? Is it treating me fairly compared to its other customers? Research by consumer psychologists has shown that customers ask these questions when evaluating the company's pricing policies and price changes. They are quick to draw inferences about fairness from what they see, and act accordingly[9].

In the case of Netflix, many customers perceived the price increase to be unfair because they felt that the company had re-

neged on its promise of leaving prices unchanged as long as subscribers maintained their subscription continuously. The lawyer
of one customer, who sued the company for raising prices, articu-
lated the individual's sense of being wronged in this way: "I can
tell you my client is upset because Netflix has acknowledged he
had a guaranteed or grandfathered account but nevertheless in-
sisted on raising his price[10]". On the other hand, Starbucks' price
increases were taken in stride by customers because they were
seen as fair, and occurring because of increases in the prices of
coffee beans and employee costs[11].

2) PRICE TRANSPARENCY

Many companies invest a lot of time and effort in making pricing decisions and executing them but have little interest in explaining the thinking behind them to customers. They wrongly
assume that customers will understand and draw the correct con-
clusions. In Chapter 4, we saw that being transparent with customers about costs and markup factors has worked well for
Costco and Everlane. What applies to the effects of cost transparency on customer reactions is perhaps even more pronounced
for price transparency.

Price transparency refers to providing customers with a detailed explanation and engaging with them in a conversation if
necessary, about the rationale for the pricing decision, and how
the price change will affect them. This is not much of a problem
when the company is cutting prices or offering incentives; but
when it is raising prices or denying a concession, this becomes
important.

Each time Starbucks raises prices, it is careful to provide a detailed and qualified explanation outlining the reasons for the increase. After one price increase, the company put out a statement saying that "Pricing is continually evaluated on a product-by-product and market-by-market basis in our stores in order to balance business needs while continuing to provide value to our loyal customers." While this sounds a bit vague, it wonderfully explains Starbucks' pricing decision-making philosophy, and customers appreciate that. The company then went on to tell customers it was raising prices to factor in higher costs of certain types of espresso beans and giving raises to store employees and managers. Finally, it pointed out that the average spending increase by a customer per visit would only be 1%, and prices of 65% of its beverages had not changed. With this sort of detailed explanation and discussion of the impact of the price increase on individual customers, customers felt fully informed and did not balk at the increase[12].

When customers are given the company's rationale for increasing prices, they feel included and part of the company, and become more open to the idea even when it is a price increase. For example, studies show that when a restaurant adopts green practices such as recycling fryer oil, installing low-flush toilets, and donating leftover food to food banks, a vast majority of its patrons are willing to pay higher prices to support these activities, even though these changes have nothing to do with taste or quality of food being served[13]. However, when these changes are made without any explanation or communication, customers will simply fail to understand why prices are higher, draw the wrong inferences and rebel against the price hike.

3) PRICE STABILITY

In addition to fairness and transparency, customers also value price stability. Imagine if you walked into a grocery store and put a gallon of milk priced at $3.99 in your shopping cart. A few minutes later, when you have completed your shopping and are checking out, the cashier rings up $4.15 for the milk. When you wonder why, the cashier tells you, "Oh, don't worry. The prices of milk went up while you were shopping." How will this make you feel?

A colleague recounted an airline ticket buying experience where this very thing happened to him. He frequently flies for work and often books tickets under the wire. Because he is a Platinum frequent flier, he calls a dedicated customer service line reserved for the airline's most profitable customers to book his tickets. When he called this time, he was quoted a certain price, $X. As the reservation agent was entering his credit card number to confirm the reservation, she muttered, "Oh shoot! Wait a minute. I cannot believe it. They just changed prices. You will now have to pay $Y, not $X".

When prices are unstable, customers find it hard to form a range of reasonable prices for the product, and their decision-making process becomes more complicated. Instead of making a quick evaluation, they have to think carefully about whether the price is a good one or not. Under these circumstances, people delay making a decision or back out of it altogether[14]. For example, when the price of a jacket, handbag, or a pair of shoes fluctuates many times every day on an online retailer's site, the best option for many shoppers is to simply tune out and postpone the purchase.

Another negative consequence of constantly changing prices is that it shifts the customer's attention away from the product's features to its price[15]. People are hard-wired to pay attention to stimuli that change and ignore the ones that remain stable. When prices change continuously and the product's other features do not change at all, consumers naturally turn their attention away from the features that provide them with functional and hedonic benefits and focus their attention on its price, something that goes against the grain of sound marketing practice.

FAIRNESS, TRANSPARENCY, AND STABILITY MATTER IN PRICING DECISIONS

Few managers give much thought to the issue of how customers will react to the company's pricing decisions. As we have seen, it is important for the company's pricing to be fair, transparent and stable. Customer reactions can make or break pricing decisions if they are not considered, planned for, and handled correctly by the company. Just calculating the most profitable price is not enough. For success, customer satisfaction with pricing decisions and the company's pricing policy is essential. It is something you should consider and monitor as part of making and executing sound pricing decisions.

WHAT EMPLOYEES WANT FROM PRICING DECISIONS

Customers are not the only people affected by the company's pricing decisions; they also have significant effects on employees. After a pricing decision is reached, frontline employees are responsible for its implementation. They are the ones on the line if price execution is bungled in some way, and they are the people who have to answer to customers and deal with the backlash. Employee involvement and support is essential for successful pricing.

To see why this is the case, let's consider Netflix again. As part of its transition from a DVD rental company to a streaming video company in 2011, it decided to raise its subscription prices by around 60%. Notably, it did not ask for any customer feedback before rolling out this price increase. What is worse, hardly any employees were consulted either[16]. The decision to raise prices was top down. The company's CEO Reed Hastings, along with members of his top management team drove the price increase.

After the increase was announced, however, while the executives were (figuratively) back-slapping each other, Netflix's public relations team and customer service representatives bore the brunt of customers' anger and frustration. Thousands of subscribers made their feelings known in no uncertain terms through social media and by calling the company. By the time this fiasco was over, Netflix had lost over 800,000 subscribers, and its stock price was down by 75% from before the episode started. Within a year, four of the company's top managers had departed.

This case provides noteworthy lessons. When a firm makes a significant pricing decision, especially one to increase prices, the frontline employees such as the salespeople, PR spokespersons, customer service representatives, and account managers have to deal with customer reactions. They have to communicate the increase to customers, suppliers, and investors, explain the rationale behind the change, deal with resistance and blowback, which is sure to come, answer questions, negotiate with customers using the revised prices, and try to excel at price execution.

Despite the importance of these tasks to the price increase's success, managers rarely consider how pricing decisions will affect frontline employees. This is a real area of opportunity to improve your company's pricing performance. Far too many companies perform poorly simply from not considering the issue adequately. The inclusion of frontline employees who deal with customers on a daily basis is of particular importance as the following case studies illustrate.

THE AFTERMATH OF A CEO CHANGE AT A CERAMICS PRODUCTS MANUFACTURER

Not too long ago, one of my students worked for a manufacturer of decorative ceramics products that were sold in high-end home goods retailers. The company produced different lines of high-quality, premium ceramics that were in high demand at the time. Shrewdly, the company rarely discounted anything. In fact, it had not run a single price promotion for its trade channels in years. It managed to build and retain a strong portfolio of loyal customers and enjoyed steady revenue and profit growth year after year. Then its longstanding CEO, who was also the company's founder, retired and was replaced by a company outsider.

One of the first things the new CEO did was to revamp the company's pricing strategy. Abandoning the strategy of steady growth and a zero discounting policy, the company's new unspoken mantra became "aggressive growth at any cost." The quotas of everyone on the sales team were increased substantially, and they were encouraged to offer discounts to their customer accounts to ramp up sales and to beat competitors' prices. They were assured that even after offering these incentives the company would still make a healthy profit. How do you think these changes affected the morale and performance of the company's sales staff?

When the company sold its products at full price, the salespeople had a healthy sense of pride in its product lines. They were imbued with what pricing experts Reed Holden and Mark Burton call "a little arrogance[17]." However, when the emphasis changed to aggressive discounting with little explanation from the top, salespeople were filled with confusion and doubt. They did not know why such excellent, in-demand products were suddenly being discounted so heavily. From their original position of strength in negotiating and taking orders from longstanding customers, they were now in a position of weakness even when they approached customer accounts they knew well. Instead of describing how good the products were, and pointing out their strengths, the salespeople spent most of the time in their sales calls discussing prices and talking about the depth of discounts on offer. The result was a markedly greater turnover in the sales ranks and deteriorating sales performance. As time passed, the company's brand was tarnished. It could never regain its firm footing in the high-end home goods retail channels.

FRONTLINE EMPLOYEES DICTATE THE SUCCESS OF A GROUPON PROMOTION

In 2010 and 2011, the daily deal site Groupon was on fire. It became the fastest company to reach a billion dollars in market valuation, achieving this milestone in less than two years[18]. Local small and medium-sized businesses such as restaurants, salons and spas, and yoga studios started running daily deal promotions through Groupon and its dozens of competitors. Offering deep one-time discounts (usually 50% off regular price) seemed like a good way of bringing in new customers, and earning revenue using the short-term price floor that we discussed in Chapter 4. However, many businesses failed miserably with running Groupon promotions[19].

One big reason for the lackluster performance was unhappy frontline employees. Many Groupon promotions were for upscale products and services that are rarely discounted, such as helicopter-flying lessons, hot yoga, and artisanal chocolate. As a result, the companies offering the cut-rate pricing with a Groupon or another daily deal site had little or no experience with running this type of price promotion and specifically dealing with bargain hunters who are drawn to it. They were inadequately prepared for who would come and how they would behave. Managers did not train frontline employees or prepare them for the onslaught of penny-pinching customers, nor did they adjust how the employees would be compensated during the promotion.

Without such preparation, these businesses faced the same issue as the high-end ceramics manufacturer. The frontline employees could not decipher the rationale behind offering high-quality, premium products and services at bargain-basement prices. For instance, one business owner who had run Groupon promotions told me, "Some [of my employees] were reluctant to understand the benefits and thought we should not be giving away the product for so little."

Even worse, many frontline workers were hurt where it counted the most, which was in their paychecks. Many new customers who came in to redeem daily deals failed to tip adequately, using the full billed amount. Instead, they tipped on the deeply discounted amount. Many businesses did not compensate their employees for the shortfall, further increasing their frustration. In reporting this research, my conclusion was[20]:

> "Overworked or skeptical employees are less able (or inclined) to create a positive customer experience. Their behavior can make the Groupon offer backfire, since two keys to reaping profits from the coupons are getting the Grouponers to buy items in addition to the discounted one and to become repeat customers who will pay full price in the future. In fact, preparing employees for upcoming promotions and obtaining their buy-in is the most important factor influencing a Groupon promotion's success: Employees at businesses where the coupons generated profits had a 63% higher satisfaction rate, regarding how they viewed customers than employees at businesses where the promotions failed."

Both cases illustrate the importance of involving employees, especially those who are on the frontline, in the company's pricing decisions. You can do this by encouraging them to obtain customer feedback to use in pricing decisions, by explicitly providing them with the rationale behind the decision, and by linking their compensation to a slate of outcomes that include profit and customer satisfaction instead of sales growth alone. Let's consider each of these ideas in more detail.

1) Empower Frontline Employees to Obtain Customer Feedback and Execute Prices.

The first, and perhaps the most impactful, step in encouraging frontline employee cooperation is to actively involve them in making pricing decisions. Far too often, I have seen managers only think about the financial payoff of pricing decisions, and ignore the softer, people-based factors entirely. This is a shame. Because they interact with customers constantly, frontline employees often have the most accurate and comprehensive understanding of how customers will react to the price change. They can help gather information about the pricing decision inputs from customers, in particular, the drivers of customer value and reference prices being considered by customers. An academic study conducted by Horace Melton and Michael Hartline with over 160 services organizations found that involving frontline employees and customers in the design and development of new services led to a more efficient process for developing innovations and resulted in greater sales of the new services when they were introduced[21].

For pricing decisions, frontline employees can not only collect and share insights obtained from customers, but they can also help to test the effectiveness of different price presentation options and deliver the most efficient price cues to customers at the point of purchase. In some situations, frontline employees can even play an active role in setting prices. For instance, many Starbucks baristas are allowed to make original drinks that customers request or that are born of their creativity and charge a price that is consistent with the other products[22]. As we saw in

Chapter 8, this kind of autonomy has a positive impact on both employee morale and their job performance[23].

2) EXPLAIN THE PRICING RATIONALE TO FRONTLINE EMPLOYEES.

Strong price execution relies on good communication just as much as it does on sound calculations. Explaining the rationale behind the pricing decision to frontline employees serves two purposes. The first one is purely informational. It gives them the information they need to do their job, such as answer customer questions and provide service more efficiently. Secondly, it is a source of empowerment because once employees understand the reasons and goals for the price change, they can support these objectives more expertly. In my research of businesses running Groupon promotions, the biggest complaint of frontline employees was they did not understand why such deep discounts were being given to customers. The lack of information was like a black hole that drained their motivation and preparation, left them befuddled, and lowered their job performance.

When a small business owner or manager assembled everyone and explained that the goal of the Groupon promotion was to introduce new customers to the company's products, and cross-sell other higher-margin products, suddenly the confusion disappeared, and employees felt more prepared. As consultancy PwC suggests, such explanations need to include both rational arguments ("We need new customers to maintain a healthy level of profit") and emotional arguments ("It is exciting to have a full house on otherwise slow days")[24]. Providing clear and complete explanations gives frontline employees clarity about the company's pricing policies.

3) LINK EMPLOYEE COMPENSATION TO PRICE EXECUTION AND CUSTOM-
ER SATISFACTION RATHER THAN TO SALES GROWTH ALONE.

Pricing experts point out that perhaps the most damaging aspect of a focus on sales growth is that employees at the frontline
take their attention away from other measures that matter to the
company's long-term health. They will do whatever it takes to
close the sale because that is what senior managers emphasize is
the priority. Such a mentality is exacerbated by compensation
schemes that institute quotas and reward volume sold without
any consideration of profit margin earned from the sale. For
frontline employees, the path of least resistance to a high
paycheck is to keep offering incentives to customers until they
purchase. After all, it does not cost the employee anything and
fattens their paycheck.

A continued trend to deal with this serious problem is to in-
corporate other outcome measures into the formula to calculate
employee pay and incentives. Research suggests that linking part
of employees' compensation to profit margins, customer satisfaction, and customer behaviors that are indicative of strong relationships such as repurchases and referrals is beneficial. One
insurance company links 20 percent of the performance pay of its
frontline employees to achieving preset customer satisfaction
targets. According to a senior executive at this firm, "The programs work well since the company has enshrined customer satisfaction in its corporate vision and value statements[25]." Along
similar lines, pricing experts argue that it is crucial to link a significant part of bonuses to the average profit margin earned from
the sales, rather than to the sales volume. This encourages em-

ployees to consider discounts negatively and to be thrifty with incentives to customers during the sales process.

THE IMPORTANCE OF ENGAGING FRONTLINE EMPLOYEES IN PRICING ACTIVITIES

In the battle for pricing excellence, employees are the foot soldiers that can make or break the pricing strategy. You should pay attention to how employees react to pricing decisions, and enlist their assistance in serving the company's best interests for the pricing decision to work. Now, in the final part of this chapter, we will consider the case of the Indianapolis Zoo. It provides an excellent case study about how an organization can successfully and innovatively balance different pricing outcomes to attain pricing excellence.

HOW THE INDIANAPOLIS ZOO EVALUATES ITS PRICING PERFORMANCE

As a rule, zoos are not renowned for their innovative pricing strategies. Zoos are non-profits, run by managers who are more interested in conserving wildlife, maintaining animal health, and increasing appreciation for the wonders of the natural world than they are in using cutting-edge pricing methods.

Most zoos use a simple, two-tiered fixed price structure with adult and children's tickets. Many zoos also have free or half-off prices one day each week to provide access to the community. In contrast Indianapolis Zoo, the country's largest privately funded zoo[26], has taken a more innovative approach to pricing. Since the summer of 2014, buying a ticket to go there has the same type of variability as buying an airline ticket to fly to Indianapolis (with some significant differences, as we will see).

VARIABLE, DEMAND-DRIVEN ENTRANCE TICKET PRICING

The Indianapolis Zoo scrapped its rigid ticket price structure and adopted a variable pricing model to correspond with the opening of its new $30 million Orangutan exhibit. The zoo's managers were concerned that the new exhibit would draw a quarter of a million visitors over the summer holidays, leading to overcrowding on weekends and an unpleasant experience for visitors[27]. They wanted to manage attendance levels with their ticket prices and saw variable pricing as the way to do this. The new pricing structure even had a catchy slogan: "Pick your day, pick your price, pick your package." It was the first zoo in the United States to adopt variable demand-driven pricing[28]. Three years later, it remains the only zoo in the country using it, although some other zoos are seriously considering its adoption.

The zoo's variable pricing structure works as follows. Entrance ticket prices are calculated for each day based on projected attendance, expected weather, whether it is a holiday, whether it is a weekend and other factors. Customers can buy tickets online or at the zoo's ticket counter at any time at the stated price. To encourage online purchases, ticket prices are lower online than they are at the gate. As tickets are purchased, depending on the demand and proximity to the visit day, prices keep increasing, just as they would for an upcoming airline flight. Unlike other industries that use variable pricing, ticket prices never go down; they can only go up or remain the same. This assures customers that they will never be penalized for buying tickets in advance. As the zoo's marketing director Dennis Woerner told me, "Plan ahead and pay less. The highest attendance price is always going to be on the same day at the gate."

The zoo's previous fixed ticket pricing model was conventional. Adult tickets cost $16.95, and children's tickets cost $11.95 during the peak season from Memorial Day to Labor Day. Off-season tickets were $10 for adults and $8 for kids. After variable prices were instituted, ticket prices vary on a daily basis, are set in advance, and updated daily. The price differences are significantly greater, with a range of $8-30 that was imposed by the zoo's managers. For example, an adult ticket on a Tuesday in March could be purchased for $10.20, but the price was $24.45 for a Saturday in July.

To help people decide when to visit, the zoo's website displays a calendar with projected attendance using a color-coded scheme[29]. Days highlighted in green have the lowest prices; those marked in red are expected to have heavy attendance and the highest prices.

The zoo's primary objective for changing to variable pricing was to shift demand from weekends to weekdays. The zoo's managers had observed that when attendance hit a threshold of ten thousand on any given day, visitor experience dropped steeply in quality and complaints increased significantly. To evaluate its new pricing method, one metric the zoo used was the number of days in the year when more than ten thousand people visited. (They wanted to lower this number and spread attendance to other days). Additionally, the change from fixed prices to variable rates amounted to a hefty price increase. Thus the zoo monitored effects of the price increase on revenue and attendance numbers.

HOW SUCCESSFUL WAS THE ZOO'S VARIABLE TICKET PRICING?

The results of the change in pricing strategy were impressive. By adopting variable pricing, the Indianapolis Zoo was able to shift approximately 10% of its visitors from weekend to weekday visits during the peak summer months. This reduced the number of 10K+ visitor days from 40 down to 10, resulting in improved customer experience for thousands of visitors. Considering the attendance and revenue metrics, in 2013, with the old fixed ticket pricing, the Indianapolis Zoo had a total attendance of 1,029,800 (including members who did not have to buy a ticket for each visit), and admission revenue per attendee of $6.63[30]. The corresponding numbers in 2015, the first full year in which the zoo used variable pricing, were an attendance of 1,205,400 (an increase of 17%) and admission revenue per attendee of $6.84 (an increase of 8%). Under normal circumstances, an increase in attendance at a zoo (or another comparable venue) is matched by reduced revenue per attendee. It occurs because of more free access days. However, for the Indianapolis Zoo, both attendance and revenue per visitor metrics increased at a healthy rate after variable pricing was introduced.

LESSONS FROM INDIANAPOLIS ZOO'S PRICING STRATEGY

The Indianapolis zoo's adoption of variable pricing and its choice of measures to assess pricing success provide useful insights and lessons for every organization.

1) GOOD PRICING DECISIONS OFTEN DO NOT START WITH A PARTICULAR PROBLEM. INSTEAD, THEY BEGIN WITH A MINDSET OF IMPROVEMENT.

The Indianapolis Zoo was doing fine and did not have a serious problem that needed fixing. Nevertheless, the zoo's managers adopted a "let's improve" mindset to enhance visitors' experience even further. This is particularly impressive because zoos, like many non-profit organizations, tend to be managed conservatively with a "don't rock the boat" mentality. Even considering, let alone adopting an innovative pricing method that was unproven in the industry, and vastly complicated was a significant risk. For the zoo's managers, it was a "strange risk to do this, and a leap of faith[31]." Its main lesson is good managers are always looking to use pricing strategy to improve their business performance and get a leg up on competitors. Not only is pricing a powerful profit lever, but it can also be a strong differentiating lever and a business-model-improvement lever. In the case of the Indianapolis Zoo, it has been all things.

2) BE CLEAR ABOUT THE PURPOSE AND ESTABLISH PERFORMANCE METRICS TO EVALUATE THE PRICING DECISION BEFOREHAND.

The zoo was clear in establishing its purpose for switching from fixed to variable prices. While its managers desired a revenue increase, it was not their priority. The zoo's focus was to manage the demand for its services, and shift visitors from weekends to weekdays in the summer, and thus improve customer experience. Thus, it judged the success of its new pricing through counting the number of 10k+ visitor days and the number of customer complaints.

3) CONSIDER EMPLOYEE SATISFACTION EXPLICITLY AND PREPARE EMPLOYEES FOR POTENTIAL ISSUES BEFORE THE PRICE CHANGE.

The zoo's employees were concerned about backlash from the sticker shock some visitors would experience with the new variable prices. Specifically, complaints from some visitors who had to pay $25 at the gate when they were used to paying $17 before were expected in the first few months after the variable pricing took effect. The zoo's marketing director prepared its frontline employees, and as a group, they had the poise to hang on through the initial anxiety and concerns. Within a few weeks, customers got accustomed to the new pricing, and it became a non-issue.

4) SUPPORT THE PRICING DECISION WITH CONSISTENT MARKETING AND SALES PROGRAMS.

When rolling out the new, more complicated pricing structure, the zoo took some steps to facilitate visitor understanding. When the pricing change was made, a full-fledged marketing communications program was launched to explain the new pricing scheme's flexibility ("Pick your day, pick your price, pick your package"). It emphasized the fact that it would reward early planners by lowering their prices, and encouraging them to buy tickets online instead of at the gates. The website was revamped to provide detailed information about how the pricing scheme worked. With these moves, the zoo explicitly paid attention to, and managed, customer reactions to the price change.

5) LOOK OUTSIDE YOUR INDUSTRY NORMS FOR INNOVATIVE ANSWERS
TO YOUR PRICING QUESTIONS.

Perhaps the most impressive aspect of this case study is the willingness of the zoo's managers to look for a pricing approach far outside its industry. In my experience, this is a rare occurrence. Most managers tend to look within their peer group of companies when considering possible solutions to pricing problems. For instance, one oil field services company will benchmark its pricing against other oil field services company, and builder will imitate other builders. Instead of looking at other zoos, Dennis Woerner talked to major league baseball teams and concert halls to understand their experiences with variable prices, and to gauge potential effects such pricing could have on the zoo. Such a broad outlook is something every manager should consider when looking for effective pricing ideas for their organizations.

CHAPTER SUMMARY

In this chapter, we saw that the success of pricing decisions should be assessed by a combination of outcomes that includes sales, profit, customer satisfaction, and employee satisfaction. Such a balanced approach of assessment will result in more successful and sustainable pricing strategies for the company. Sales, and particularly sales growth, is the most commonly watched and tracked measure of pricing performance because it is readily influenced by temporary price changes, and provides some diagnostic information about the company's financial health. However, paying attention to it alone often gives a distorted view of pricing performance and the company's health. Including profit as an outcome measure allows the organization to understand and focus on customers that derive the most economic value from its products, and use pricing tactics that increase profit instead of growing the customer base and sales volume indiscriminately.

In addition to these two financial measures, people-based measures are important considerations. Customer reactions to a price change can determine its success or failure. Customers want fairness, transparency, and stability from the company's prices and pricing policies. When one or more of these qualities is lacking, there is potential for backlash that can undermine the organization's pricing activities. Finally, frontline employees also need to be considered and included in pricing decisions. They should be empowered to obtain customer feedback and execute prices and be told the rationale for the pricing decision. Where possible, employee compensation should be linked to metrics such as earned profit margin and customer satisfaction rather than to sales alone. The main point to take away from this chapter is that managers should avoid focusing on sales growth alone, and give greater weight to profit, customer satisfaction, and employee satisfaction in assessing the effectiveness of pricing decisions.

[10]

PRICING BUSINESS PRODUCTS

How hard for real worth to gain its price. – Edward Young

In business markets, value-based pricing has a specific con-
notation and a mythic reputation. B2B marketers distinguish between three pricing methods. We have already
studied two of them in detail. With the cost-plus method covered
in Chapter 4, the company estimates its costs and forecasts sales
as accurately as possible and then calculates the price by applying
a markup factor to these costs. When using comparative framing
discussed in Chapter 7, the company sets prices relative to key
competitors. It may set prices higher if it wants to be viewed as a
premium supplier, and at a lower level if its objective is to be a
low-cost provider for price conscious customers.

One company that I know uses this simple rule: Get the prices
of Competitor A's products from its new annual catalog and add
a dollar amount (and for some products, a specific percentage) to
calculate its prices for the year. This is an extreme version of
comparative framing. Whether pricing higher or lower than the

competitor, the primary goal of comparative framing is to maintain price stability and to avoid price wars. Every company has a
"price location" in the market and keeps it year after year. This is
why businesses that use comparative framing intelligently don't
deviate too far from their competitors' prices. However, imitation
is not a strategy. Using this method means ceding any strategic
thinking about pricing decisions.

The third method in business markets is the value-based pricing method in which customers' economic valuation of the product is assessed carefully and then used to set product prices.
Although it shares a common name, the value-based pricing
method discussed in this chapter is different from the *value pricing framework*. The *value pricing framework* is a structured
method that considers multiple decision inputs and balances conflicting outcomes to make effective pricing decisions. The B2B
value-based pricing method, on the other hand, is a focused
method that calculates the differentiated economic value of a
product to business customers, which is then used for making
pricing offers and in negotiations.

Mostly, B2B pricing experts agree that the value-based pricing method is superior to the cost-based and comparative framing pricing methods, and will lead to more effective pricing for
B2B companies[1]. Such a positive assessment is because value-
based prices are usually higher and are derived from hard evidence about the product's differentiated economic value. With
proper documentation, the information gathered, compiled, and
analyzed during value-based pricing gives salespeople the am-
munition to offer a credible and persuasive explanation for their
price quote to customers.

THE BEST PRICING METHOD IS THE LEAST USED BY B2B COMPANIES

While most B2B companies aspire to use the value-based pricing method, in reality, few companies do so. In his comprehensive survey documenting the use of different pricing methods by B2B companies from 1983 to 2006, Andreas Hinterhuber found that almost half of them primarily used some form of comparative framing to set prices. Another 37% used cost-based methods, and only 17% used the value-based pricing method. Hinterhuber's research leads to the startling conclusion that the very method of pricing that is widely regarded as the most useful is also used by the fewest number of B2B companies.

On a hot sunny summer afternoon, when you are driving on a highway, have you seen a mirage? It appears shimmering in the distance and seems just within grasp. However, as you keep rolling, it keeps receding. In my experience, value-based pricing is a lot like this mirage. When discussing pricing, B2B managers are always saying they will use value-based pricing to price their next product or their next big deal. It never happens. They continue to use their status quo pricing method whether it is based on costs or competitors' prices, giving away a significant portion of their product's economic value to savvy, hard-nosed customers.

The good news is that value-based pricing is not difficult to understand or use once its purpose and the steps involved in it are well understood. Instead of thinking of this method as a way to discover and set the perfect price, a more realistic way is to think of value-based pricing as a tool to calculate defensible prices for use in pricing discussions with customers.

In this chapter, we will carefully review each step in the B2B value-based pricing method, and dispel key misconceptions that many managers have about it. This chapter's goal is to provide you with a clear understanding of how to use the value-based method for pricing any business product. We will also consider the case of Pfizer Oncology's pricing of its breast-cancer drug Ibrance, which provides a particular application of value-based pricing. First, we begin with a brief discussion of the philosophy on which the value-based pricing method is based.

THE PHILOSOPHY BEHIND THE VALUE-BASED PRICING METHOD

In the 1970s, when marketing scholars were considering the best way to describe the basis of ethical marketing practice, they settled on the concept of exchange[2]. To this day, the American Marketing Association defines marketing as a set of processes that facilitate the exchange of value between buyer and seller. The idea behind marketing as exchange is simple. The company produces and delivers the product to the customer. In return, the customer pays the company. Each party chooses to participate in this transaction voluntarily, offering something the other party values, and receiving something they consider to be of equivalent value in return. Both sides walk away satisfied, and hopefully, go on to participate in future exchanges.

For an exchange transaction to occur, both parties must agree to its terms and determine the product's value. Here's where things can get tricky in business markets. The buyer can see the product, ask for a trial, conduct tests, or obtain recommendations from third parties with expertise or experience. With one or a combination of these methods, the buyer evaluates the product's value and determines whether its valuation equals or exceeds the seller's asking price.

However, the assessment process is far more difficult for the vendor, who has to figure out exactly how much the buyer values the product. Estimate too low a number, and you have left money on the table, and give the buyer a good deal. Determine a number that is too high, and the buyer will walk away. Since the beginning of civilization, sellers have resolved this dilemma by haggling in some shape or form. When the buyer and seller meet, the seller starts the process with a "high-ball" offer in a bid to gauge the buyer's valuation. The two parties trade offers of the amount the seller wants, and how much the buyer is willing to pay. Offers and counteroffers are traded back and forth, and eventually the buyer and seller settle on a mutually acceptable price.

In consumer markets, we do not haggle anymore (at least not in the Western world). Fixed take-it-or-leave-it prices have made that impossible. Just try walking into Whole Foods, filling your shopping cart with groceries, walking up to the cashier and trying to haggle with him, "Sell me this piece of chocolate cake for $3, $5 is too much, I refuse to pay that much." It will not be long before law enforcement arrives, and from there, things could get rather unpleasant for you.

Unlike consumer products, much of the B2B world today continues to operate as if it were a medieval bazaar. What used to be called haggling a few centuries ago is now called negotiating. The buyer and the seller meet (physically or virtually), make their opening offers, argue back and forth and end up with a price that is acceptable to both parties.

This is where the value-based pricing method comes in. The seller needs a reasonable way to determine what its opening offer should be. It also needs evidence-based arguments to support its asking price and to deter the buyer from talking it down. Consider the following thought experiment. Let's say you use a cost-based pricing method. In the negotiation process, your opening bid will go something like this: "It cost us $25,000 to make this machine, which is why we are asking you for $30,000." If you use comparative framing price instead, your explanation will be: "Competitor A is asking you $32,000, which is why we are asking you for $30,000." From the buyer's perspective, neither of these explanations sound particularly coherent or persuasive. Estimating the product's economic value to the customer, and using this estimate as a starting price in the negotiation process makes much more sense.

There is one significant difference between the medieval customers of eight or nine centuries ago and your customers (besides, let's hope, better personal hygiene). Today's B2B customers have an excellent understanding not just of your product's features, but they also know a lot about your competitors' product features and prices. This makes it impossible to consider customer valuation of product features in any absolute sense, as we discussed in Chapter 5. In business markets, the product's value has to be calculated and communicated relatively, in terms of its superiority or inferiority over other alternatives.

The question for your company is, "To help our negotiations with the customer, how do we calculate a logical, evidence-based, and defensible price reflecting the economic value derived by the customer?" The value-based pricing method allows you to do this.

DEFINING THE VALUE-BASED PRICING METHOD

Let's begin with our definition of the B2B value-based pricing method, then discuss each step of the process in detail: ***Value-based pricing is the method of price determination by which the company calculates and tries to earn the differentiated economic value of its product for a particular customer.***

This value-based method has six steps that are illustrated in Figure 10.1. In step 1, you will start by identifying the target customer account or segment. In step 2, you will determine the competitive offers that the customer is interested in, and identify the "focal competitor" or the closest alternative to your product. In step 3, you will conduct a head-to-head comparison, and in step 4, you will identify your product's differentiators and deficiencies relative to the focal competitive offer. In step 5, which is the most critical step, you will assess the differentiated economic value of your product. Finally, in step 6, you will calculate the value-based price of your product.

Figure 10.1 The B2B value-based pricing method

To understand each step in the process, let's use the example of a commercial display monitor manufacturer who wants to price its latest LED display using the value-based pricing method. In this example, let's assume that Brand A is a leading commercial display brand that is about to introduce a new 80-inch model. It will be the first commercial display of this size in the market. It wants to determine the display's asking price.

STEP 1. IDENTIFY THE CUSTOMER

We saw in Chapter 5 that value is customer specific. Value specificity is particularly important for pricing in business markets where customers often use the same product as an input or ingredient into vastly different processes having different economic value or resell the product using different business models. As an example, quick-drying paint has a superior economic value in a marine application such as painting a boat. Here the paint's quick-drying property translates into significant time and labor cost savings, compared with painting the interior of a commercial building where its quick-drying property may not generate savings. A naval shipyard and a builder will therefore be willing to pay significantly different prices for the paint and should be treated as different customer types by the paint manufacturer.

The first step of the value-based pricing method is to identify which customers you are targeting for the pricing decision. As the paint example illustrates, B2B customers fall into segments[3] based on shared similarities in economic value derived from the product, their buying decision criteria, and processes, and the factors they consider to be of significance in price discussions.

One oilfield services company I know has three customer segments. Its marketing and sales organizations distinguish between nationally-owned oil companies like Saudi Aramco, Gazprom, and Petrobras, the major diversified multinational oil companies

such as Exxon Mobil, BP and Chevron, and the small independent oil producers like Anadarko, Chesapeake Energy, and Murphy Oil. For pricing purposes, it treats each segment separately
and calculates a value-based price for each one. The economic
value derived from the products and services, which competitors'
offerings are considered, the power dynamics between the company and its customer, and how the negotiation process is conducted are all significantly different for the three customer
groups. B2B companies also distinguish between customers based
on other criteria such as their level of prior experience with the
customer, the size of the account, and so on. The main point here
is that value-based pricing is a customer-specific method because
economic value is customer specific.

In our commercial display example, based on differences in
buying criteria, the manufacturer also identifies three customer
segments: (1) small and medium-sized businesses that purchase
1-5 displays directly through its website, (2) larger organizations
such as retail and restaurant chains that purchase larger display
quantities directly and are serviced by salespeople, and (3) distributors, who purchase displays for resale. Let's assume that, for
the purpose of this example, the manufacturer is interested in
calculating the display's value-based price for its small and medium-sized business segment.

STEP 2. DETERMINE THE COMPETITIVE OFFER SET AND THE FOCAL COMPETITOR

When making purchase decisions, B2B customers do not consider just one option. They usually examine a handful of choices
seriously before choosing one. To form this consideration set,

many B2B organizations use processes such as a request for proposal, a request for quote, and a request for tender (in the case of government contracts). These methods are slightly different from one another in how they work, but their primary purpose is to identify a subset of suitable options that can be considered in detail before making the final choice.

Understanding which competitive offers the customer will consider along with the company's offer is a crucial part of using the value-based pricing process successfully. Once the particular competitive offers that the firm is up against are known or identified, it helps to establish the comparison baseline against which the customer will evaluate the product. In the value-based pricing process, it is common to pick two to four other competitive offers that are serious contenders, research their relevant features, and create a comparison table describing them, along with the values of the company's product and competitive offers.

The Focal Competitor

To make the task of eliciting the features and their economic value more manageable, a common approach is to identify a single "focal competitor" from the customer's perspective. The focal competitor is the competitive product that the customer considers the closest viable alternative to the company's product. Some pricing experts call the focal competitor the "next best alternative." However, I avoid using this term in this book because it implicitly, and misleadingly, conveys the idea that the company's product is superior to its competitors. In reality, the focal competitor can be formidably superior, significantly inferior, or virtually identical to the company's product in its features and delivered value. In cases where the company has an established relationship with the customer, the focal competitor might even turn out to be the previous generation of its product or a superior product from its product line that the customer cannot afford to purchase.

While this winnowing makes the value elicitation task more manageable, it has one limitation. Sometimes, it is difficult to identify who the focal competitor is. Many B2B customers may themselves not know the final two options in their consideration set until deep into the purchase decision process. If the company waits, the value-based price may cease to be useful for negotiation. It is much easier for the customer, and more realistic, to identify the two or three competitors that are in contention and provide details about these competitive products early on in the decision-making process. Another way to solve the problem of identifying the focal competitor is to use the judgment of experienced managers. One specialty chemicals company that I know routinely uses multiple methods including intelligence from key account managers and the knowledge and "gut feeling" of senior executives to identify the focal competitor relatively early on in its discussions with individual customers.

Returning to our example, the display manufacturer will conduct research with its small and business-sized business customer accounts and use the judgment of its managers based on experience to narrow down two significant competitors (Display B and Display C). Let's assume it identifies Display B as the focal competitor against which its target customers will evaluate the company's new display monitor (see Figure 10.2).

Features	Display A	Display B	Display C
Brand	A	B	C
Backlight	LED	LED	LED
Definition	4K Ultra HD	4K Ultra HD	4K Ultra HD
HDMI Inputs	4	3	3
Built-in Wifi	Yes	Yes	Yes
Refresh rate	240 Hz	240 Hz	240 Hz
Smart TV	Yes	No	Yes
Warranty	3 years	2 years	2 years
Screen Size	80 inches	70 inches	65 inches
Price	??	$3,199	$3,349

Company → Display A

Focal competitor → Display B

Figure 10.2 Comparison of features of competitive commercial display monitors

STEP 3. CONDUCT HEAD-TO-HEAD COMPARISON OF YOUR PRODUCT WITH THE FOCAL OFFER

This step is the heart of the value-based pricing process and involves the most amount of work. It requires the company to gather information about its product features and competitors' features that are relevant to the customer. Particular attention is given to the focal competitor's product to make sure that its features and pricing is understood accurately. For our example, Figure 10.2 provides a comparison of the three displays on their key features. As can be seen, many features are standard for the three display monitors in the table. All three displays are backlit with LEDs, have 4K Ultra HD image quality, and built-in Wifi.

To obtain this information, B2B companies use one or more marketing research methods. The display manufacturer may question buyers of its larger customers, talk to its distributors, or hire an independent consultant to conduct a market analysis. Nowadays, in many business markets, obtaining this information is simply a matter of doing a thorough internet search. Most companies or their channel partners provide detailed information about product features online. Information about prices is a bit trickier to find.

STEP 4. IDENTIFY DIFFERENTIATORS AND DEFICIENCIES

Once the comparison chart describing the product's features, its focal competitor, and other competitors is developed in step 3, the company assesses where it stands relative to the focal competitor. The features on which it outperforms its focal competitor are called "value-added differentiators." These are the same as points of superiority in Chapter 7. They are features with the potential to earn a price premium. On the other hand, there may be other features where the focal competitor performs better. These features are labeled "deficiencies" or points of inferiority (in Chapter 7) indicating that the company may have to offer the customer a discount relative to the focal competitor's price.

Returning to the display's pricing, the company's Display A, and its focal competitor Display B, are equivalent on many features. They are LED displays, have 4K Ultra HD definition, built-in WiFi, and a refresh rate of 240 Hz. The chart shows that Display A has four value-added differentiators and no deficiencies. Its value-added differentiators are that its screen size is 80 inches (vs. 70 inches for Display B), its warranty of 3 years (vs. 2 years), 4 HDMI inputs (vs. 3 inputs for Display B), and the Smart TV feature (which Display B does not have).

Why include additional competitive products in this comparison beyond the focal competitor? The answer is to obtain guidance regarding how the customer may value the differences in other features. In our example, notice that one fundamental difference between the two competitive displays, B and C is that Display C has the Smart TV functionality, whereas Display B does not. Even though Display B is larger than Display C (70 inches vs. 65 inches screen size), Display C is still priced $150 higher than Display B ($3,199 for Display B, and $3,349 for Display C), suggesting that Smart TV functionality is a valuable feature for customers.

STEP 5. ASSESS THEIR ECONOMIC VALUE

Perhaps the most misunderstood aspect of the value-based pricing process is the process by which the product's economic value is evaluated. As we saw in Chapter 5, any product or service has an indeterminate number of features. It is unrealistic to expect any method to be able to assess the economic value of every single characteristic. Fortunately, we do not need to do this. We only need to determine the economic value of the differences from the focal competitor.

In the example, the display manufacturer would only need to assess how much more money customers are willing to pay for the bigger screen size (80 inches vs. 70 inches), one extra year of warranty (3 years vs. 2 years), one additional HDMI input (4 vs. 3), and the Smart TV functionality.

Specific customer-focused research to obtain this information would require either careful customer interviewing or value-in-use research. Typically, an early adopter is given the product at a subsidized rate in exchange for letting the company study how they use the product, and the cost savings and the revenue generation opportunities presented by its value-added differentiators and deficiencies.

In B2B companies, two standard methods to calculate these values are by conducting and documenting credentialed value case studies and by using value calculators. In both cases, by cooperating with customers, the company establishes the superior quantifiable economic value delivered by its product relative to the alternative, whether it is another competitor's offering, the previous version of the company's product, or a solution that has been stitched together from a number of different suppliers. Let's consider both methods briefly.

CREDENTIALED VALUE CASE STUDY

One way to discover and document the differentiated economic value of the product is to cooperate with one customer and carefully understand its economic value in the field when an actual customer is using the product. This information is then made available as a business case to salespeople. The product's greater economic value may accrue from cost reductions relative to the competitor's offer (e.g., simpler or quicker assembly that saves labor costs, fewer materials or cheaper ingredients saving material costs, more streamlined design requiring fewer parts, etc.) or better performance (e.g., faster operation, longer life, less downtime, etc.). In exchange for "signing off" on the product's superior economic performance, the customer usually gets special perks or benefits. These can include reduced pricing, prioritized access to new products in the future, a discount on service plans, or special standing in a user group of customers.

Value calculator

A value calculator is a spreadsheet-based or web-based app that salespeople, technical staff, consultants, or customers use to calculate the differentiated economic value derived from the company's product. Value calculators allow detailed calculations covering both initial purchase costs to the customer, and ongoing costs of product operation, service, maintenance, and training. For example, Siemens Healthineers offers customers of its imaging equipment a set of tools to calculate the total cost of ownership of the product. Customers can quantify and compare the value of Siemens' products to other vendors on such dimensions as technical and applications support, advanced engineer training, remote repair, on-site response times when the product breaks down, and protection from obsolescence through automatic software and hardware updates through the duration of the service contract[4].

Let's say that with these methods, the company in our example finds out that the value is $750 for the larger screen size, $125 for the HDMI input, $200 for an extra year of warranty, and $250 for the Smart TV functionality.

Step 6. Calculate the Value-Based Price

Once the differences of the product are quantified, the output is the product's value-based price. For the display monitor, the net premium of the differentiated features is $1,325 ($750 +

$125 + $200 + $250) over Brand B's price. Thus, the value-based price of Display A is $3,199 + $1,325 = $4,524.

In most cases, the value-based price is not the final price. Instead, it provides the initial starting point for discussions with the customer. From this value-based price, downward adjustments are made to account for customer relationship, environment, and competitive factors. Various incentives are also offered, as we saw in Chapter 8. A simple heuristic is to share the value premium 50-50 with customers. In a strong economic environment with high customer demand, the company may try to keep more of the premium for itself. When the market is weak, the company may be hard-pressed to keep any of the value premium at all, as we saw in the Toyota Prius case in Chapter 3.

There is usually a significant gap between the differentiated economic value and the product's price. This gap is a function of the company's pricing power in the marketplace, the significance of its differentiation to the customer, the availability of alternatives, and so on. According to venture capitalist Tom Tunguz, startups are typically only able to capture 10–15% of the differentiated economic value they create[5]. When the company is larger and more established than its customers are, it may be able to earn as much as 50-60% of the generated differentiated value.

DISPELLING KEY MISCONCEPTIONS ABOUT THE VALUE-BASED PRICING METHOD

Value-based pricing is used or considered for use today in virtually every business market, from software, bridges, and drugs, to cement, oil rigs, and aircraft. Because it is such a widely discussed and aspirational pricing method in B2B circles, there are

also many misconceptions about how it works. Fully understanding and then dispelling these misconceptions here is important
for you to be able to use this method effectively. Let's discuss the
most common misconceptions about the value-based pricing
method.

MISCONCEPTION #1. VALUE-BASED PRICING REQUIRES YOU TO EVALU-ATE AND ESTIMATE THE CUSTOMERS' WILLINGNESS TO PAY FOR EACH PRODUCT FEATURE.

Many B2B marketers erroneously believe that when a company uses value-based pricing, it has to evaluate how much the customer values every single product feature, assign a dollar amount
to it, and then add them all up to calculate the product's final
price. Even the simplest B2B products have dozens of value-
adding features. Just imagine the difficulty of pulling this procedure off for an oil rig or a tractor, or a cloud-based software program. This misconception turns many managers away at the
outset from even considering the value-based pricing method, let
alone using it for pricing. They are happy to estimate their costs,
mark them up by a reasonable factor, and then call it a day.

In reality, the features that the product has in common with
the customer's status quo, such as the previous generation of the
company's product or a particular competitor's offering, is cap-
tured by its price. In the display monitor example, for instance,
the fact that both displays have LED backlights, built-in Wifi, a
refresh rate of 240 Hz, and 4K Ultra HD is included in Brand B's
$3,199. Brand A's manager does not have to calculate each fea-
ture's economic value separately. The only thing they have to do
is identify its feature differences relative to Brand B and then as-

sess customers' valuation of these differentiated features. Because fewer features are involved, this method is a lot easier to implement than it seems. However, it also exposes an overlooked, but potentially serious weakness of this pricing method.

MISCONCEPTION #2. EVEN IF YOUR COMPETITORS ARE DUMB WITH THEIR PRICING DECISIONS, USING VALUE-BASED PRICING WILL ALLOW YOU TO EARN A PROFITABLE PRICE.

This is likely the most dangerous misperception about value-based pricing because it can create high expectations that are entirely unfounded in reality. Many B2B managers consider value-based pricing to be a panacea to all their pricing woes. If they use it, they believe, they will improve their profit margin under any circumstances. This is not the case. Its success depends on how intelligently competitors have priced their products, and on the company's past pricing decisions. If competitors have set untenably low prices, the value-based pricing method cannot do much. The same thing applies to a company that has traditionally priced its products using cost-based methods with small markups. In both cases, the customer will evaluate the current product's price using reference points of the company's previous prices or the competitors' prices. They will only be willing to pay a premium for any differentiated, improved features, not for all the features that the product shares in common with its previous version or with its focal competitor.

To understand this limitation, just imagine what would happen if Brand B foolishly chose to sell its display for $1,499 instead of $3,199. Brand A would still only be able to charge the $1,325 extra for its differentiated features, and no more. Therefore, instead of charging $4,524, it would have to charge $2,724, ending up with a significantly lower price than it merited. It may perhaps even lose money solely because its competitor Brand B has made a poor pricing decision.

The conclusion is inescapable. In any competitive market, a company cannot make good pricing decisions unilaterally. Competitors within its industry also have to make good pricing decisions and price intelligently if value-based pricing is to work successfully. The same logic applies to a company that is shifting from using cost-based pricing that gave away a lot of economic value to a value-based pricing method that is geared to identify and keep more of this value. Customers will not just take hefty price increases overnight. The shift must be done gradually, with patience, using a step-wise method over a period of multiple pricing cycles for it to work effectively.

MISCONCEPTION #3. YOUR BRAND'S VALUE IS PART OF THE VALUE-BASED PRICING CALCULATION.

With value-based pricing, the manager's goal is to assign a dollar value to every differentiating feature. The method's focus is on features that give value to the customer and which can be converted into dollars and cents. Features such as "longer-lasting by X%," "faster by Y hours," "less likely to break down by Z%," all match this focus because they can be converted into monetary values. However, it is a lot harder to turn a brand's value into money. This is why the brand value is usually left out of the equation with value-based pricing, or given little weight. This is also one reason why this method is mainly used in business markets that traditionally give less weight to the brand.

SUMMARY

Value-based pricing is an effective way to price business products. On the one hand, it is a lot easier to implement in practice than it appears. You will only need to identify and assess your product's differentiated features, not every feature. However, it is not a panacea. When competitors have priced their products foolishly, the value-based pricing method will not be of much use. With a stronger grasp of how this process works, you will be able to make smarter pricing decisions and employ value-based pricing as a way to set evidence-based prices to use for negotiations with customers. Next, we will work through an in-depth case study to understand how companies use value-based pricing in practice.

PRICING A NEW DRUG WITH THE VALUE-BASED PRICING METHOD

Ibrance (palbociclib) is an FDA-approved medication for women with metastatic breast cancer. It belongs to a class of therapies called CDK 4/6 inhibitors, that, when combined with hormonal therapies, has proven to be effective in halting the progression of certain forms of metastatic breast cancer[6]. Ibrance was launched in the US market in February 2015 by Pfizer Oncology. The case study of how its price was determined provides an inside look into how companies use value-based pricing.

COVERING COSTS AND IDENTIFYING ECONOMIC CUSTOMER VALUE

As soon as the chemical compound from which Ibrance evolved showed initial promise in clinical trials, Pfizer Oncology's marketing team started thinking about what its price would be. This thinking began as early as November 2011, more than three years before the drug was launched[7]. Unlike many drugs that are priced by the dose, pill, or tube, cancer drugs are priced by the month, specifically, by how much a month's supply of the medications will cost. At this stage, the company's focus was not on determining Ibrance's final launch price but rather in deciding whether a business case could be made for launching the drug in the first place. The company considered its costs of development along with the criterion of whether there was a reasonable chance that it would be able to cover the R&D costs (see our discussion of this process in Chapter 4).

Pfizer Oncology's marketing team also started investigating possible reference prices. They wanted to identify a range of competitors and their offerings. Once the competitors were known, their prices were easy to find. Given the market's distinct niche, the company did not need to perform much competitor analysis at this stage. Similarly, the demand for the drug, if it could be developed successfully, was well understood.

For this exercise, the marketers gathered prices of several other comparable cancer drugs. They found that on average, medicines in this domain were priced at approximately $10,000 per month. With this rough price estimate in hand, and after assessing the likelihood of FDA approval, Pfizer Oncology decided to continue studying the drug's efficacy.

IDENTIFYING KEY REFERENCE PRODUCTS WITH A MULT-STAGE PROCESS

As encouraging signs regarding the drug's effectiveness continued to come, the company interviewed oncologists and cancer public health experts. On this basis, they identified one widely used but older cancer drug called Herceptin as the focal competitor. Herceptin's price was \$4,775 per month, considerably lower than the initial \$10,000 price estimate. As this shift illustrates, with value-based pricing, the choice of reference competitor can affect the pricing decision significantly.

Pfizer Oncology also expanded its understanding of customers by conducting qualitative research. They conducted hour-long in-depth interviews with 125 oncologists in six US cities to understand their prescription behaviors. Through this research, they identified three additional competitive products that were important references: Kadcyla and Perjeta by Roche and Afinitor by Novartis AG. These drugs ranged between \$9,000 and \$12,000, again in the ballpark of the initial \$10,000 estimate.

More than a year before launch, Pfizer started fine-tuning its pricing strategy and pinning down its multiple conflicting goals. While the company wanted to earn significant revenue from the drug, it also wanted to ensure that most patients would be able to have access to it. This meant that Ibrance was not priced at a level where health insurance companies would avoid it. For this drug, as for any prescription medication, insurers are gatekeepers because they pay a significant portion of the drug's price.

CONDUCTING MORE GRANULAR CUSTOMER RESEARCH AND ESTABLISHING THE LAUNCH PRICE

A year before launch, Pfizer did yet more customer research. It surveyed 80 health-plan experts including medical directors of hospitals and pharmacists. They were asked about the suitability of price levels between \$9,000 to \$12,000 for Ibrance, and the point at which they would start to get reluctant and require further monitoring and evidence of efficacy before approval. These interviews revealed that $11,000 was a significant price resistance threshold. The research also discovered there would be a 25% drop in prescriptions at a price above $10,000. Using these findings, Pfizer set Ibrance's launch price at $9,850 per month.

SUPPORTING THE PRICE WITH MARKETING ACTIVITIES

To support the $9,850 per month price, the company developed a complete package of collateral materials for insurance companies that gave information about Ibrance's clinical benefits and risks and its effect on their budgets, given estimated consumption rates of patients. The collateral also included information about current treatment costs and ancillary spending such as treating infections, and expenditure on the patient in the absence of the drug's benefits to make a stronger case for the lower total cost of using the drug compared to its competitors rather than a price comparison alone. This approach of supporting the asking price by providing an estimate of total cost of product use is a hallmark of using value-based pricing.

POST-LAUNCH PRICE INCREASE

Five months after its launch, a study by pharmacy benefits manager Prime Therapeutics found that Ibrance's price rose by approximately 8% to $10,669 per month[8]. The number of healthcare practitioners who prescribed the drug grew 33% from 3,000 to 4,000 during the three months from June 2015 to September of 2015, while the number of patients treated with Ibrance grew by 66%, from 9,000 to 15,000. These adoption rates were higher than forecasts made by Pfizer Oncology as well as industry analysts[9]. This evidence pointed to the initial price decision as being effective and also refutes the conventional wisdom held by many B2B marketers that raising prices after introducing new products will not work.

PRICE DISCRIMINATION IN OTHER MARKETS

When Pfizer launched its drug in the United Kingdom, it set the price at $3,700 per month, approximately one-third of its price it the United States. Interestingly, it could earn a profit even at this price. However, UK's National Institute for Health and Care Excellence found this price to be far too high and unjustifiable for use in its National Health Service. It rejected the drug. Cancer patients in the UK could still use the drug, but they would have to pay for it out of pocket, ruling out all but the most affluent patients from using it. There are two lessons from this incident: (1) value-based prices have little to do with costs, and (2) different customer segments derive varying levels of value from the same product, so value-based prices must be customized to customers.

LESSONS FROM THE IBRANCE PRICING CASE STUDY

The process used by Pfizer Oncology in pricing Ibrance meets many of the criteria of the *value pricing framework* developed in this book. While it applied the value-based pricing method, the company also implicitly considered all four pricing decision inputs, costs, customer value, reference prices, and the value proposition, carefully from early stages of its development. It considered R&D expenses in the initial stages when making the decision of whether to proceed with developing the drug. Manufacturing costs were trivial to the ultimate price of the drug as it focused strictly on customer value and reference prices[10]. Customer value was considered by extensively interviewing oncologists, public health experts, and insurance company personnel. The company set initial prices carefully to remain within the range of reasonable prices, changed the price smartly after launch, and applied price discrimination between markets. Throughout, Pfizer Oncology stated that its goal as not to maximize profit, but to balance the revenues from the drug's sales with providing access to the drug to more of the cancer patients who could benefit from it. In the company's case, greater access meant more revenue.

CHAPTER SUMMARY

In this chapter, we gained an in-depth understanding of the value-based pricing method in business markets. While it is superior to the other two widely used methods by B2B companies, cost-plus, and comparative framing pricing, value-based pricing is still an aspirational practice for most companies and is not in widespread use. The goal was to provide a practical guide so that you can start using this method.

We used the definition, "Value-based pricing is the method of price determination by which the company calculates and tries to earn the differentiated economic value of its product for a particular customer" and studied the six steps involved in implementing it. In step 1, the company identifies the particular customer or segment for which it wants to calculate the price. In step 2, it determines the competitive offers of interest to this customer, and identifies the "focal competitor" or the closest alternative to the product. In step 3, the company conducts a head-to-head comparison of its product and the focal competitor. In step 4, it identifies the product's differentiators and deficiencies relative to the focal competitor. In step 5, the most critical step, the company assesses the product's differentiated economic value. In step 6, it calculates the product's value-based price.

The value-based price provides the initial starting point for discussions with customers. From this value-based price, downward adjustments are usually made to account for the company's pricing power, and for the environment and competitive factors. A simple heuristic is to share the value premium equitably with customers, but the actual proportion of sharing is a function of the company's pricing power in the marketplace, the significance of its differentiation to the customer, the availability of alternatives, and so on. We also considered and dispelled three common misconceptions about value-based pricing in business markets that may prevent its adoption or lead to misplaced expectations about its use, and we discussed the case study of how Pfizer Oncology priced its cancer drug Ibrance using this method.

[11]

PRICING CONSUMER PRODUCTS

She loved expensive things because she knew what their expensiveness meant. She had a complete understanding of the signifiers. – John Lancaster

Imagine there is a food truck called Star Hot Dogs. It is rated as one the best food trucks in the country, with thousands of five-star Yelp reviews from gushing hipsters. Star's owner has adopted a clear and compelling value proposition for his business, "to provide inexpensive and delicious late-night fare for the bar and club-going crowd," and is executing it brilliantly. The truck operates every day from 6 p.m. to 3 a.m. in a buzzy part of town, with many bars and clubs. It is extremely popular among college students and young urban professionals. During peak weekend hours, it is hipster heaven, drawing long lines of hipsters snaking around the block, who are willing to wait more than an hour.

Star Hot Dogs sells a single product. The "Everything Dog" comes with six carefully curated toppings such as pickled onions and balsamic mustard that synchronize to create an amazing flavor. The Everything Dog costs $4, and customers are actively discouraged from asking for customized toppings because it slows the line. The truck also sells Coke, Sprite, and bottled water for $1 apiece.

Although business is great, the operator has some concerns. On a recent weekend, when a popular concert in a neighborhood venue brought even more foot traffic than usual, he raised the hot dog's price to $6 without any explanation. This impromptu increase did not go over well with customers. A number of them posted scathing Yelp reviews slamming the owner for price gouging. He also wonders whether he is pricing too low and whether he could be earning more money from selling one of the hippest hot dogs in the country. If you applied the *value pricing framework* to Star Hot Dogs, what recommendations would you give the owner to solve these problems?

APPLYING THE VALUE PRICING FRAMEWORK TO STAR HOT DOGS' PRICING PROBLEMS

From a strategic pricing perspective, it is clear that the owner is doing many things well. He covers his costs easily, and his gross margins are more than 100%. The truck has a compelling value proposition that has resulted in a successful business. However, using the *value pricing framework* terminology, his pricing challenges can be framed in this way: (1) Customers have an unyielding, single reference price point of $4 for the product, making it tough to increase prices, and even worse, (2) the owner is not able to raise prices even during peak hours or on peak days. Here are two changes that will help alleviate these problems.

1) SELL A GREATER VARIETY OF PRODUCTS, OFFERING VARIATION IN FEATURES AND PRICES.

This recommendation is one major theme of this chapter. Selling a single, specially configured hot dog to deliver the optimal taste at one price has benefits. It is simple to communicate to customers and to assemble on the food truck. However, this simplicity comes at a high price, no pun intended. It creates a very strong reference price point of $4 making it difficult to break away from it. More problematically, with the "single product–single price" model, the business loses opportunities to take more of the economic value that is generated during peak times.

The best way to solve this problem is to change the single reference price point to many reference prices, that is, a range. To do this, the owner will have to increase the menu's complexity. He can do this in many ways. One way is by offering a menu of three or four different hot dogs at various prices. A second way to accomplish this without adding to the complexity of food preparation, assembly, and sale, is to create three or four different hot dog recipes (or what pricing experts call "versions") with various toppings and give them different names[1]. Then the owner could choose to sell one of them every evening. Importantly, the prices of these hot dogs would be different, ranging from $4 to $6.

Providing variety across different days would increase unpredictability and generate excitement and anticipation even among the truck's die-hard customers. Moreover, such an approach will change the reference price of regular customers from a single number ($4) to a price range ($4-$6). Then the owner can simply sell a more expensive, higher-margin hot dog on a peak day, and a cheaper one on a non-peak day, without enraging customers. This method provides fairness, transparency, and stability to the food truck's prices, characteristics that are valued by customers.

2) OFFER COMPLEMENTS AND PREMIUM DRINKS.

When people are peckish and buy a hot dog after a long evening of socializing and carousing, they are in the mindset of impulsive consumption[2]. Chances are they will be receptive a bag of chips or Cheetos. Similarly, instead of offering only three drink choices at $1 each, the owner should consider adding a premium tier of drinks—Red Bull, bottled iced coffee, and packaged fruit juice at $3–4 apiece. The idea behind offering complements and premium drinks is to sell more of the high margin products to the same customers with no additional preparation or labor costs. The higher the average ticket per customer, the greater will be food truck's profit margin.

HOW PRICING IN CONSUMER MARKETS DIFFERS FROM BUSINESS MARKETS

As this mostly-fictitious case study illustrates, pricing in consumer markets is entirely different from B2B pricing that we considered in the previous chapter. First, many consumer purchase decisions are made on-the-fly, with very little deliberation or explicit comparisons. Instead, consumers' habits and lifestyles are important[3]. On the one hand, people tend to buy things they are familiar with and have preferred in the past. In contrast, even when they like a particular brand, they are prone to seek variety across purchase occasions and choose a different option just for the sake of trying something new[4]. The company's prices have to support, and even encourage consumer decisions that are made on the fly, and dictated by habitual and variety-seeking shopping tendencies.

Second, prices play dual, contradictory roles in consumers' buying decisions. High prices both attract and repel customers. In some instances, the price will be used as a signal of quality (as described by the Emery model we studied in Chapter 5) so that consumers may flock to the $4 hot dog as a gourmet snack option when heading home from the club. On the other hand, a high price can also be a turn-off, when consumers pay attention but cannot discern quality differences between the different priced options, or when they are extremely price conscious. Managers need to weigh the attracting and repelling abilities of high prices where their products are concerned.

The third important difference in consumer markets is that the brand is a significant, and often the biggest driver of customer value. It is often the main reason why customers are willing to pay a price premium and here, it need not be backed fully by actual quality. The fact that Star Hot Dogs was named among the best food trucks in America recently and has thousands of five-star Yelp reviews boosts its image and increases customers' willingness to pay more to eat one of its unique hot dogs than they would at another food truck. Unlike business markets, a consumer company's marketing strategy has to understand and monetize the brand's value and use pricing to strengthen the brand and enhance its value.

In this chapter, we will consider three pricing methods that address these unique challenges of consumer markets. Pricing decisions in consumer markets must accommodate both the differences between customers in their preferences and valuation, and in their inclinations to prefer habitual and lifestyle-driven purchases. To provide variety and choices to consumers, the company must explicitly acknowledge that their customers are different from each other in their preferences and desired benefits. In fact, even the same shopper may have different preferences on separate occasions, preferring to splurge on one occasion, but be very price conscious another time.

We will study the use of good-better-best pricing (also known as assortment pricing) that allows the company to offer choices to customers to account for their heterogeneous preferences[5]. We will consider the value of price bundling, which is one of the most attractive pricing methods for consumer products. It allows the company to deliver value in customized ways. Third, we will consider how habitual and lifestyle-driven buying behaviors of consumers can be supported through subscription pricing by automating repetitive purchasing processes.

GOOD-BETTER-BEST PRICING

For several decades now, marketers have developed and offered different products to different customer segments. While this method of making segment-based offers, which relies on differences in tastes, preferences, and personalities of customers, is still widely used by marketers (just look at any brand of cars or shoes), a simpler approach is to offer a line of products that vary in price and quality and let customers decide. Instead of targeting specific segments, the idea behind good-better-best pricing is to allow customers to self-select into the segment they want. Figure 11.1 illustrates this pricing method.

With good-better-best pricing, the company systematically offers different versions of the product to the same customers based on how much they value the product and the level of benefits they want on a particular purchase occasion. The good option in the product line is low in price and quality, the better option is medium price–medium quality, and the best option is the premium option, with the highest quality and price.

For example, someone flying for work may buy a business class airline ticket when her company is paying for it. On another occasion, however, she may settle for the cheapest middle seat in coach when traveling for leisure. The benefits sought by the customer in the two cases are completely different, and she will choose different versions of the product.

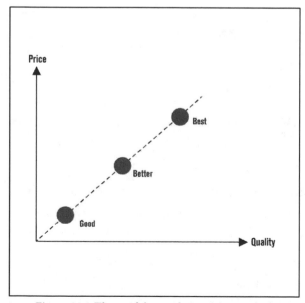

Figure 11.1 The good-better-best pricing method

THE GOAL OF GOOD-BETTER-BEST PRICING IS TO ENCOURAGE CUSTOMERS TO TRADE UP.

With good-better-best pricing, the manager's goal is to motivate customers to trade up from the good option to the better option, and from better to the best option. By offering different choices, at the first blush, it may appear that the manager has shifted the decision of which version to buy to the customer. However, the truth is that through both subtle and overt methods, the marketer can influence customers to purchase the more expensive option than the one they had in mind to begin with.

Take the example of buying pork chops in the supermarket. Stores often use good-better-best pricing, publicizing a deal on thin-cut pork chops (the good version) in newspaper ads and signs in the store at a mouthwatering price. However, when the shopper reaches the meat case, the thicker-cut (better) and pasture raised organic chops (best) are displayed right next to the thin chops. In such a line-up, the thin-cut chops will not seem as appealing to many shoppers, and they will gravitate towards a pricier option. The goal of encouraging an overt comparison using a carefully designed display case is to lure buyers towards more expensive choices by demonstrating their superior value at the point of purchase. Kent Harrison, marketing VP of Tyson Fresh Meats describes the logic in this way[6]: "Retailers must make sure to stock their case with a variety of choices, to give consumers the option of moving up to the next tier of quality, which will also be an opportunity for the retailer to gain higher total dollar sales." And in many cases higher margins as well!

TRADING UP IS FACILITATED BY ON-THE-FLY CONSUMER DECISION MAKING.

Once customers have made up their minds to purchase a particular product category, it is much easier to influence their decision about which specific item to buy. This is because individuals routinely change their minds at the point of purchase[7]. Often, the situation itself may make the trading-up decision an easy one. For example, if someone else is paying for the airline ticket, upgrading to premium economy or business class makes sense on a long-haul flight. Alternatively, the individual may be at a bar and having a splendid time with friends. At such a time, ordering a top-shelf drink instead of a cheaper rail drink feels like a natural upgrade. Or they may justify the expensive choice to themselves in other ways—"I do not buy a new car every day, so I might as well opt for the pricier version with the bigger engine and the all-wheel drive."

Pricing expert Rafi Mohammed provides an interesting example of Southwest Airlines introducing a "Business Select[8]" fare in which customers paid $10 to $30 more, and received amenities such as priority boarding, faster passage through security lines, and a coupon to exchange for an alcoholic drink. In evaluating the introduction of this best option, Mohammed estimated that it increased Southwest's revenue by $100 million and operating profit by 10% in the year after it was introduced[9].

WHEN CUSTOMERS TRADE UP, THE COMPANY EARNS A HIGHER PROFIT MARGIN.

The reason companies push customers away from the good option towards the better, and best options is simple. In most cases, the good option is the company's bread and butter. Close to 90% of passengers fly coach, and this is where most of an airline's revenues come from. A majority of vehicle buyers purchase the base version of the car or truck. Most travelers book the standard room on a hotel property. The good options are core products that are sold to the company's core customers, covering its costs and allowing it to stay in business year after year. Not surprisingly, companies are conservative about pricing good options. They cannot afford to lose their core business, so they will usually restrict prices, and profit margins for these products.

When offering better and best options, however, such pricing conservatism is not necessary. Customers who are interested in more expensive choices are also less price sensitive. They are conscious about non-price factors such as appearance, comfort, status, style, and performance. Companies can sell the better and best options at higher profit margins. Take the case of airline seats. On a flight from New York to London, an economy ticket may cost around $900; the premium economy tickets are priced at $1,800 to $1,900 while a business class ticket costs $4,000-5,000[10]. The additional cost of offering the marginally greater legroom, better meals, and free alcoholic beverages in the premium economy and business classes are not proportionally higher. The airlines make higher profits from these upgraded seats[11].

THE VALUE OF GOOD-BETTER-BEST PRICING FOR THE COMPANY

In consumer markets, it pays to give customers choices that vary in quality and price. This was something the food truck at the beginning of this chapter did not do. Giving customers the ability to choose between good, better, and best options of the product has significant advantages. Instead of trying to figure out a particular customer's value grid, providing a range of choices allows customers to act on their occasion-specific value perceptions and choose the option that is the most appealing to them. Providing options also makes the company appear responsive and inclusive. In addition, designing methods to influence customers at the point of purchase by steering them towards the better or best options is an effective way to improve performance on multiple pricing outcomes. Providing premium choices and encouraging customers to upgrade is the key to the success of the good-better-best pricing method.

PRICE BUNDLING

Price bundling is another of the most popular consumer pricing methods. It refers to the sale of two or more separate products or services in a single package that is offered at a discount relative to the prices of the individual items. There is no integration of the bundled products in a price bundle, but the issue of what constitutes an individual item is important. For bundling to be a meaningful incentive to customers, each product or service in it must have its market that is independent of other products. Thus, a retailer can bundle a laptop and a carrying bag because each can be sold and used separately. However, bundling a CPU, plastic case, and computer screen don't make much sense. These components have little use by themselves. As a result, price bundling provides no additional benefits to the consumer beyond what is provided by the individual products. Its primary value is in the money saved because of the bundling discount.

There is also a second type of bundle called a product bundle, in which multiple products and services are integrated in some way and then sold together. The integration provides customers with additional benefits. In some cases, the benefits can be substantial. A classic example of a product bundle is a mutual fund, in which combining a number of individual stocks in a portfolio reduces the buyer's risk and allows them to meet specific objectives such as generating income, investing in emerging markets, and so on.

Where price bundling is primarily a pricing method to provide more choices to consumers, product bundling is strategic in nature. Price bundling can be performed efficiently, costs little, and may be offered for a short duration. Product bundling, on the other hand, is a long-term differentiation strategy of the company that is approached from a new product development perspective. In this chapter, we will focus on price bundling.

EXAMPLES OF PRICE BUNDLING

Price bundling is practiced in virtually every industry in some shape or form. Here are some examples of bundled consumer products and services.

1) An internet service provider offers a package of services including web access, email, a browser, instant messaging, and web hosting for one monthly price.

2) A premium bank account is a combination of separate checking and savings accounts, a debit or ATM card, a credit card, access to investment advice, retirement planning, insurance products, and currency transactions. Each one of these products and services has its own market.

3) During Houston Restaurant Weeks every August[12], many local restaurants offer prix fixe dinner menus, bundling an appetizer, main course and dessert for $35 or $45, a much lower price than the individual prices of the items. They donate $5 to the Houston Food Bank. This promotion is highly successful. It raises millions of dollars for the food bank, and it brings a steady stream of new customers to the restaurants.

4) A round-trip airline ticket is a bundle of two one-way tickets. Travel agents offer bundles of travel packages that include airport transfer, car rental, hotel accommodation, and activities at the tourist destination such as museum visits, tour guides, performances and meals in tiered packages.

HOW PRICE BUNDLING BENEFITS THE COMPANY

Perhaps the most useful benefit of price bundling is to reduce costs. This occurs in multiple ways. First, when done correctly, price bundling reduces the company's inventory cost. For instance, automaker Chrysler's decision to cut down its minivans to a single model called Pacifica, and offer only five bundles of pre-assembled accessories or trims such as the LX, Touring, and Limited significantly reduced its cost of holding different model configurations in inventory[13]. The second type of cost reduced by bundling is the seller's sorting cost, which is passed on to its channel members or customers. An example is a storage facility operator that auctions off entire storage lockers to intrepid consumers to recover unpaid rent, instead of selling each locker's contents, as seen on the popular television show Storage Wars[14].

A third way in which price bundling reduces costs is by providing greater economies of scale and scope. When a software maker develops and then sells multiple products together (Microsoft with Office, Outlook, and Internet Explorer, or Google with Gmail, Google Calendar, and Google Docs), its development costs are reduced. These savings can be significant when the products have low marginal costs and high creation costs such as software, movies, and music. On the other hand, for products with high marginal costs of production such as the typical consumer electronics product or appliance, the cost savings from bundling will be lower. Fourth, selling bundles instead of individual products reduces marketing expenses, especially when the customer must purchase the bundle, and cannot buy individual constituents a la carte.

Another benefit of price bundling to the company is to serve as a segmentation tool that allows customer segments with different product valuations to buy a product bundle that maps on to their respective valuations. This benefit is similar to good-better-best pricing, where customers self-select the option that they like most. It also accounts for the diminishing marginal valuation of many products. A single ticket to a baseball game, concert, or a Broadway show has a higher price than the per-event season ticket price. A six-pack of beer costs less per bottle, and the per-unit price of a case is even lower when compared to buying a single bottle. The company's sales are higher because of offering the bundle. We will examine this issue in more detail later on.

Price bundles take into account the fact that many customers prefer variety but have neither the wherewithal nor the inclination to pay full price for this variety. Thus, an appetizer platter at a restaurant has a lower price than the individual appetizers in it, and a cable company offers bundles of television channels that are considerably cheaper than the same channels purchased individually.

An important value of price bundles to both buyers and sellers is that many products and services are naturally complementary. Ski rentals and ski lessons, burglar alarm kit and alarm monitoring service, and dry pasta and pasta sauce all make sense together. In these cases, selling the bundle reduces costs for the seller (as we saw earlier) and enhances the company's brand. For the customer, purchasing the bundle provides convenience. Finally, bundling also has competitive benefits. When cars are bundled with maintenance contracts, or smartphones are sold with proprietary operating systems and app stores, the bundles may make it much harder for competitors to enter the incumbent's markets.

THE THREE TYPES OF PRICE BUNDLING STRATEGIES

When offering bundles to customers, the company can use one of three distinct bundling strategies. These are unbundling, pure bundling, and mixed bundling.

Unbundling. The first strategy, which in reality is a strategy of simply not offering price bundles, is called a pure components or an unbundling strategy. In this case, the company does not provide any bundles. Customers must buy every product à la carte. There is a trend towards unbundling in some consumer markets. Online music services have unbundled many (but not all) music albums by letting consumers buy individual songs. In the airline industry, services that used to be bundled a few years ago are now unbundled by many airlines. These include checking in luggage, in-flight meals, and assigned seating.

Unbundling makes sense in situations where customers value each unbundled product or service sufficiently, and when they are provided at high marginal costs. Unbundling is also supported by social psychological research, which shows that when prices are unbundled, customers tend to evaluate each aspect of the product or service more carefully and provide higher service evaluations[15]. In most cases, however, providing a price bundle of some sort is a more effective strategy.

Pure bundling. Pure bundling is the diametrically opposite approach to unbundling. In this case, the company only offers the bundle for purchase. Individual products cannot be purchased separately. European ski resorts and Caribbean beach resorts only offer one-week packages during peak times like the holidays. Weekend or single night accommodation is not available. Pure price bundling can also be used to achieve specific strategic objectives. For instance, by creating a pure bundle that included the Internet Explorer web browser, Microsoft succeeded in increasing its share of the web browser market from virtually nothing in the mid-1990s to over 90 percent a decade later[16]. Similarly, Pfizer sought to bundle its heart transplant drug Torcetrapib with Lipitor, its best-selling cholesterol-lowering drug. Its logic was that creating a pure bundle would extend its pricing power for Lipitor even after its patent expired[17]. Finally, pure bundling is sometimes used to sell distressed inventory. In the case of hotel rooms or airline tickets, the respective companies sell soon-to-expire rooms and seats in bundles to intermediaries such as Priceline and Hotwire at a substantial discount. The risk of selling them shifts from the hotel or the airline to the intermediary.

Mixed bundling. With the mixed bundling strategy, customers can buy the bundle (usually at a discount) or some of the individual products in the bundle. Patrons can purchase different menu items at a fast-food restaurant, or a combo meal bundle at a discount. In some instances of mixed bundling, customers often pay full price for the primary product, which is usually a cutting-edge, attractive product, but receive a discount for the secondary product, which is generally less appealing or differentiated. They may even have to buy the bundle just to avail of the primary product. For instance, the only way to buy a ticket to see the popular Broadway show, Hamilton, in Austin Texas is to subscribe to the entire Broadway season of six shows. While single tickets to other shows are available for purchase, the Hamilton ticket is only available as part of the bundle[18].

A variation of mixed bundling is called value-added bundling. Here, instead of offering a discount for the bundle as a whole, the company provides additional features or services that price-sensitive customers are interested in. The discount is only available if the core service is purchased (e.g., car vacuuming as an add-on to a car wash).

WHY PRICE BUNDLING IS AN EFFECTIVE STRATEGY

Offering a price bundle is effective when the company sells products to heterogeneous customer groups that differ in how much they value each product. Specifically, when there is a "crossover" in the willingness to pay (WTP) or the valuations of the different products between the customer segments, then a bundling approach will be useful. To understand this point, let's use a simple numerical example.

Imagine a company makes two products A and B, and it has two customers segments X and Y. Further, assume both segments are of equal size. Table 11.1 provides the WTP of each segment for each product. The question is how price bundling will help the company.

	WTP of Product A	WTP of Product B
Segment X	$30	$125
Segment Y	$50	$100

Table 11.1 Willingness to pay of two customer segments

In Table 11.1, notice the difference in the WTP of the two customer segments. Segment Y has a much higher WTP for product A than Segment X ($50 vs. $30), but the pattern of valuation is exactly the opposite for Product B ($100 vs. $125). Assuming that the company's goal is to increase its product's sales, let's calculate how much money the company will earn under each of the three bundling strategies.

In the pure unbundling case, if product A is priced at $50, only Segment Y will buy it, and the company will earn $50 in revenue. However, if it charges $30, both segments will purchase, resulting in revenue of $60 ($30 each from Segment X and Y). Similarly, the revenue-maximizing price for Product B is $100. With this price, both segments will buy the product, and the company will earn $200 in revenue. Under the unbundled pricing approach, the prices to generate the highest sales are $30 for Product A and $100 for Product B. The company will earn a total of $260 from the two customer segments. The important question is: can the company earn more money than this?

The answer is yes. If the company offered a pure bundle and priced it at $150, it would earn more revenue and profit. In this case, the valuations of both customer segments for the bundle are at or below the asking price (WTP for Segment X = $30 + $125 = $155, and WTP for Segment Y = $50 + $100 = $150). Both segments will buy the A+B bundle and the company will earn $300, which is much greater than the maximum unbundled revenue of $260. Selling the pure bundle is a superior option in this case to selling each product separately.

As this example illustrates, pure bundling makes economic sense when a market has segments with different valuations for the products the company is selling. This is often the case in consumer markets. Price bundles serve to "homogenize" the value preferences of heterogeneous consumers and increase sales. In contrast, if all the segments have more or less the same valuation for the products, offering a bundle would not help.

For companies that sell a range of different products, price bundling is a powerful and effective method to increase sales. You should always consider how to use it in your company to increase revenue and to ensure that more customers buy more of your products.

SUBSCRIPTION PRICING

Another creative way of pricing consumer products is to sell with a subscription. Not too long ago, newspapers and magazines were the only products sold this way. Within the past few years, however, this has changed dramatically. Shoppers can now subscribe to virtually any product or service, from clothes and groceries to shaving supplies, pet food, meal kits, and on-demand entertainment. Tens of thousands of companies sell subscription-based products and services, and this number is growing every day[19].

Subscriptions fall into two broad types. They are either access-based or bundle-based and work as follows. Shoppers agree to pay a flat price periodically, say each month, which is automatically charged to a credit or debit card. When the subscription is access-based, customers receive access to the company's products or services and can consume them at their discretion. Examples include Netflix, cable TV, Dropbox and a gym membership. Even a car lease is an access-based subscription that gives the individual access to the car for the lease period. For a bundle-based subscription, on the other hand, either the customer asks for the item to be delivered, or the seller selects an assortment each time, whether it is casual clothing, pet food, vegan snacks, a meal kit, beauty products, and so on, and delivers it to the shopper. Examples include Amazon's "Subscribe and Save," Birchbox, and Dollar Shave Club.

WHY CUSTOMERS LIKE SUBSCRIPTIONS

For customers, the biggest advantage of buying with a subscription is its convenience. Instead of having to purchase the item each time it is needed, and sifting effortfully through numerous choices, a preselected assortment is delivered periodically. Both access-based and bundle-based subscriptions provide customers with variety that would otherwise be difficult to get. After signing up for Birchbox, for example, shoppers get a new box of different travel-sized beauty and grooming products each month. There are no repeats. Similarly, Netflix gives its customers an assortment of thousands of movies and TV shows to choose from, and gyms offer a wide variety of exercise equipment, classes, and workout options. Another benefit of subscriptions is that because the items are bundled, they cost significantly less as a whole than they would if they were purchased separately. Finally, in the case of access-based subscriptions, many shoppers simply like the idea of paying a single flat rate for access to potentially unlimited use, called the "flat rate bias."

SUBSCRIPTION IS AN EFFECTIVE PRICING STRATEGY

For a company, subscription pricing provides two significant benefits. First, it increases the amount purchased by customers and leads to an increase in sales and profit. It works by automating customer purchases. Whether it is watching a movie through Netflix or buying a box of beauty and grooming products, subscriptions convert infrequent shoppers into regular buyers who commit to purchase the product or service predictably, month after month. Subscriptions automate the buying process from start to finish, so it recedes into the background of the customer's life. The advantage of subscription pricing lies in generating a recurring, steady, and predictable source of revenue for the company. What is more, customers enjoy subscriptions, meaning that all four measures of pricing performance in the *value pricing framework* are successfully achieved with this pricing method.

One potential downside of subscriptions can counterbalance customers' convenience and enjoyment and can backfire if this pricing is not communicated and managed carefully. With subscriptions, customers lose control over the process of buying and paying for items. If they suddenly realize this loss of control, at best they may defect from the company. At worst, they will generate negative buzz in social media that could hurt the company significantly. Many publishing companies have suffered adverse effects including legal action because of not managing the subscription process correctly[20]. Every company using subscription pricing should allow customers to unsubscribe easily and clearly explain the process by which this can be done.

The second benefit of subscriptions to companies is that a majority of customers consumes less of the product than they think they will. Yet they pay the same fixed price every month for it. How many of us sign up for a gym membership resolving to go every day, yet weeks go by without a single visit? One study, conducted over three years, found that those who signed up for a gym membership paid 70% more per visit when compared to those who paid for each visit[21]. Instead of being thrifty shoppers, customers end up spending far more for the service than they would if they had purchased the service when they wanted to consume it. For the company, this is good news. With lower consumption levels, the company incurs lower incremental costs than if customers purchased the product or service when they needed it. Consequently, a significant portion of the subscription revenue goes directly to the company's bottom line.

Because of these significant benefits, virtually every company in consumer markets is either considering or has already implemented subscription pricing in recent years. This pricing method offers you the opportunity to boost revenues and profits, while providing customers with convenience and automated buying. This helps to streamline your company's revenue and build a base of customers who purchase repeatedly.

CHAPTER SUMMARY

In this chapter, we considered the distinctive aspects of pricing in consumer markets. Pricing in these markets has to account for consumer decisions that are often made without much deliberation and in the moment, and are dictated by habitual and variety-seeking behaviors. Managers must also weigh the attracting and repelling abilities of high prices and consider how to monetize and enhance their brand's value. To manage these unique challenges, we studied how to utilize good-better-best pricing, price bundling, and subscription pricing methods.

With good-better-best pricing, the company systematically offers different versions of the product to customers, allowing them to self-select the level of benefits they seek on a particular purchase occasion. Providing the choice creates the sense that the company is responsive to customers. The manager's goal becomes to motivate customers to trade up from the good option to the better option, and from better to the best option.

With price bundling, the company sells two or more separate products or services at a discount relative to individual item prices. Bundling lowers costs of carrying inventory and marketing and delivers economies of scale. It also serves as a segmentation tool to allow customers with different product valuations to buy bundles matching their respective valuations. Customers get variety at a much lower price. The real value of price bundling lies in homogenizing the value preferences of heterogeneous consumer segments.

Subscription pricing is a popular consumer pricing method, of which there are two types. With an access-based subscription, customers receive access to the company's services and can consume them at their discretion. With a bundle-based subscription, the seller delivers a pre-chosen or an assortment product automatically to the customer every period. Subscriptions provide a recurring, steady, and predictable source of revenue, automate buying behavior, and lead to greater purchasing in the product category. The overarching goal of the methods covered in this chapter is to give choices to customers in consumer markets to enable them to find products and services that will provide them with the most value.

Appendix: The Pricing Audit

The pricing audit is a structured questionnaire to help you evaluate your company's process of making pricing decisions. It covers every component of the *value pricing framework*. Answering the questions in this audit will allow you to gauge how well you are applying the principles we have discussed in this book. It will also help you to uncover potential weaknesses in the pricing process and identify areas where making changes will help improve your organization's or client's pricing decisions. The pricing audit follows the sequence of the *value pricing framework*.

When you make pricing decisions that are consistent with the principles described in the *value pricing framework*, you should be able to answer "yes" to each of the following questions. Every question where your answer is a "no" indicates a gap between the principles of the *value pricing framework* and your current pricing practices. It is a potential opportunity for improvement.

General

1) Do we know by what percentage our company's profit will increase if we can increase prices by 2% without losing any sales?

2) Are we paying sufficient attention and devoting adequate time and effort to pricing issues?

3) Do we have a structured process for setting and changing prices?

4) Is there a person or team within our company that is responsible and held accountable for making and implementing effective pricing decisions?

5) Do we pay systematic attention to the pricing environment, and consider how it will affect our pricing?

COSTS

1) When making pricing decisions, do we consider our costs?

2) Do we know which costs are incremental and which are irrelevant to our pricing decision?

3) Do we know our long-term price floor for the pricing decision?

4) Do we know our short-term price floor for the pricing decision?

5) Have we considered and designed creative pricing tactics to take advantage of our short-term price floor?

CUSTOMER VALUE

1) When making pricing decisions, do we consider customer value?

2) Do we know which product features are the most important to our customers?

3) Do we know which functional and hedonic benefits each product feature provides our customers?

4) Do we know the economic value (in dollars and cents) that the customer places on each combination of feature and benefit?

5) Do we know the total price our customer is willing to pay for the product?

REFERENCE PRICES

1) When making pricing decisions, do we consider the reference prices of our customer?

2) Do we know our customer's goal-derived category and the quality levels within it?

3) Have we determined the customer's range of reasonable prices for each level of quality?

4) Have we considered where our product's prices fall within the customer's range of reasonable prices?

5) Do we strategically supply external reference prices to our customers to influence their purchase decisions?

VALUE PROPOSITION

1) Do we think of pricing decisions in strategic terms, as consistent, synergistic, and purposeful?

2) Do we have a clearly defined value proposition for our product?

3) Is our product's value proposition differentiated, superior, relevant, quantifiable, credentialed, and sustainable?

4) Have we considered the role of price in our product's value proposition?

5) Does our product's value proposition guide us in how much weight to give costs, customer value and reference prices in pricing decisions?

PRICE EXECUTION

1) When evaluating pricing success, do we consider our price execution? .

2) Do we know which incentives each of our customers is getting from us?

3) Do we know the size of our price realization gap and the main reasons for it?

4) Do we have a plan to reduce, monitor, and manage the price realization gap?

5) Do we give your frontline employees the autonomy and incentives to care about price execution?

MEASURING PRICING SUCCESS

1) Do we pay attention to the effects of pricing decisions on our sales?

2) Do we pay attention to the effects of pricing decisions on our profit?

3) Do our customers consider our product's prices to be fair, transparent, and stable?

4) Do our employees know the rationale for pricing decisions, and do they feel adequately empowered and supported?

5) When evaluating pricing decisions, do we balance the four outcomes, which are sales, profit, customer satisfaction, and employee satisfaction?

ACKNOWLEDGMENTS

Like any other creative endeavor, writing this book has been a selfish, indulgent labor of love supported by many people. First, I want to express my profound gratitude to every one of the hundreds of Rice MBA students who have taken my pricing elective course over the past decade. This book would not be possible without them. Thanks to them, each time I teach pricing, I stumble on new facets of pricing strategy and appreciate anew just how nuanced and challenging effective pricing decision-making really is.

I also want to thank all the managers and entrepreneurs who have collaborated with my students over the years to help develop annual marketing plans for their companies. For me, enlisting and collaborating with two dozen or so companies has become an annual ritual. For my students, these projects are an excellent way to learn marketing by doing rather than talking. In the hundreds of marketing plans we have written together, more often than not, questions about pricing take center stage.

I am also obliged to my many corporate and entrepreneurial clients for giving me the opportunity to work with them. The work itself, not to mention the countless hours spent thinking about and discussing the issues involved and devising and implementing potential solutions has exposed me to a range of industries and pricing situations.

I am extremely grateful to Dean Peter Rodriguez and Deputy Dean Jeff Fleming at the Jones Graduate School of Business at Rice University, which has been my academic home since 2001.

Special thanks go to my student and graphic designer extraordinaire Dequan Jin for designing an amazing minimalistic book cover that matches my sensibilities perfectly. I am also indebted to Rohan Bairat and Mike Francis for reading the entire book carefully and providing tons of useful feedback and suggestions, and to Tony Manzur for providing thoughtful comments on Chapter 10. Thanks to my research assistant and web designer Achal Srinivasan for his able help, and to Gabby Browne for copy-editing and proof-reading the manuscript meticulously. Finally, thanks to Anita for her support, encouragement, and love.

END NOTES

CHAPTER 1 THE PURPOSE OF THIS BOOK

1. In this book, whenever I use the word "product", you should interpret it as generic shorthand for the phrase "products and services." This is because unless I state it explicitly, all the concepts, ideas, and tools in this book apply equally well to products and services.

CHAPTER 2 WHAT IS A GOOD PRICING DECISION?

1. This idea has been made famous by McKinsey's Global 1200 pricing study, which is described in detail in Chapter 1 of Baker, Marn and Zawada (2010). The full reference is Baker, W. L., Marn, M. V. & Zawada, C. C. (2010). *The Price Advantage, Second Edition*, Wiley.
2. Simon, H. (2015). *Confessions of a Pricing Man: How Price Affects Everything*, Springer. This data is discussed in Chapter 5 of the book.
3. Mohammed, R. (2010). *The 1% Windfall: How Successful Companies Use Price to Profit and Grow*, HarperCollins.
4. Michaels, D. (2012). The secret price of a jet airliner --- Discounts of 50% or more off the sticker number are common as plane makers and buyers haggle. *Wall Street Journal*, July 9. Available online at: https://goo.gl/IswcXE
5. Medical researchers Glyn Elwyn and Talya Miron-Shatz say "pinpoint[ing] the nature and characteristics of a good decision...seems an eminently feasible task but ... this first impression obscures an inherently complex and difficult task." See Elwyn, G., & Miron-Shatz, T. (2010). Deliberation before determination: the definition and evaluation of good decision making. *Health Expectations*, 13(2), 139-147.

6. Bell, D. R., Chiang, J., & Padmanabhan, V. (1999). The decomposition of promotional response: An empirical generalization. *Marketing Science*, 18(4), 504-526.

7. Ramzy, A. (2015). Blue Bell recalls all products after listeria outbreak. *New York Times*, April 21. Available online at: https://goo.gl/vE5FAl

8. Hatchimals are interactive fuzzy toy creatures that hatch out of an egg after coaxing, and require nurturing and training afterwards. They were a "hot toy" of the 2016 holiday shopping season. For more information on the pricing success of the Hatchimals, see Dholakia, U. (2017). When's the best time to buy the year's must-have toy? *Psychology Today*, January 15. Available online at: https://goo.gl/m2e3Wl

9. Dholakia, U. (2017). Five ways to shop smart and spend less on a must-have toy. *Psychology Today*, January 23. Available online at: https://goo.gl/xyfwLA

10. Marteau, T. M., Dormandy, E., & Michie, S. (2001). A measure of informed choice, *Health Expectations*, 4, 98–108.

11. Available at: https://goo.gl/57RKwJ

12. Schmalbruch, S. (2014). Here's why you'll never see Louis Vuitton products on sale, *Business Insider*, December 16. Available online at: https://goo.gl/wUigfr

13. O'Toole, M. (2016). At Everlane, transparent is the new black, *Forbes*, January 5. Available online at: https://goo.gl/RQrlgL

CHAPTER 3 THE VALUE PRICING FRAMEWORK

1. Timmer, J. (2009). Amazon decides Kindle speech isn't worth copyright fight. *Ars Technica*, March 2. Available online at: https://goo.gl/kqQr2b

2. Grewal, D., Monroe, K. B., & Krishnan, R. (1998). The effects of price-comparison advertising on buyers' perceptions of acquisition value, transaction value, and behavioral intentions. *Journal of Marketing*, 62(2), 46-59.

3. See for example, https://goo.gl/iWiqHy

4. Gardner, J. (2017). Le Cinq, Paris: Restaurant Review. *The Guardian*, April 9. Available online at: https://goo.gl/FYoISR

5. McLain, S. (2016). Toyota's Prius pays price for cheap gasoline. *Wall Street Journal*, September 6; see also, Haas, A. (2016). Hybrid sales fall with gas price. *The Philadelphia Inquirer*, September 6.

6. Personal communication with Michael Dillon, Vice President of Strategy and Analytics for the Houston Astros, April 11, 2017.

7. The source of these prices is Truecar, https://goo.gl/GUBhKe

8. *The Price Advantage* has an excellent chapter on the discrepancy between list price and realized price. In it, the authors call the realized price as the "pocket price" and provide readers with a graphical tool called the "Pocket Price Waterfall" to understand different incentives and deductions that lead to the price realization gap for a particular product or customer segment.

9. Taylor, K. (2016). Costco is staying 'Amazon-proof' as other retailers crumble. *Business Insider*, February 3. Available online at: https://goo.gl/rgWkme

10. Scuttlebutt Investor (2017). The fervent loyalty of a Costco member, February 23. Available online at: https://goo.gl/kJbKOI

11. Gordon L., & Beyman, M. (2012). Costco: Breaking all the retail rules. *CNBC*, 25 April. Available online at: https://goo.gl/Gpp4ZY

12. Dorfman, B. (2010). Target CEO sees shoppers re-emerging. *Reuters*, May 7. Available online at: https://goo.gl/MCZdAs

13. Available at: https://goo.gl/c1hni8

14. Cascio, W. F. (2006). Decency means more than "always low prices": A comparison of Costco to Wal-Mart's Sam's club. *Academy of Management Perspectives*, 20(3), 26-37.

15. Biggest grocery store markups: The worst deals in the aisles. Cleveland's Star 102 FM Radio Station, March 17, 2011. Available online at: https://goo.gl/u53GK0

16. Shapiro, N. (2004). Company for the people, *Seattle Weekly*, October 9. Available online at: https://goo.gl/sHMclL

17. Wight, D. (2009). Order in the court, *The Costco Connection*, March, 21-22. Available online at: https://goo.gl/JWlT0d

18. Wahba, P. (2016). How Costco has emerged as one of the country's top retailers. *Fortune*, October 6, Available online at: https://goo.gl/6hxZ8d

19. Moran, C. (2013). Learn the Costco price tag code to save more cash. *Consumerist*, July 18. Available online at: https://goo.gl/hB9NdF

20. Rapaport, L. (2016). Secret price codes will save you money at Costco, April 25. Available online at: https://goo.gl/cGl3EZ

CHAPTER 4 COSTS

1. Rodriguez, A. (2017). Movie studios think you'll pay crazy amounts of money to watch movies still in cinemas at home, *Quartz*, March 23. Available online at: https://goo.gl/zoGhbC

2. Govindarajan, V. (2012) P&G innovates on razor-thin margins, *Harvard Business Review*, April 16. Available online at: https://goo.gl/iHTh0O

3. Byron, E. (2010). Gillette's latest innovation in razors: The 11-cent blade, *Wall Street Journal*, October 1. Available online at: https://goo.gl/Eu7FcX

4. Woodyard, C. (1990). Taco Bell rings in new price setup. *Los Angeles Times*, October 30. Available online at: https://goo.gl/EnSPe2

5. Nagle, T., Hogan, J. & Zale, J. (2011). *The Strategy and Tactics of Pricing, Fifth Edition*, Prentice Hall. This book has an excellent and much more detailed treatment of the incremental costs in Chapter 9.

6. Interestingly, Justin Bieber gets the performance royalty from radio stations because he co-wrote the song, not because he performed it. However, he's a variable cost to Spotify on both performance and song-writing counts. A good explanation of the process of performance royalty payments is given in Consor, K. (2014). What you didn't know about radio royalties, *Songtrust*, August 14. Available online at: https://goo.gl/dPgSkC

7. Kempner, T. (1960). Costs and prices in launderettes. *Journal of Industrial Economics*, 8(3), 216-229.

8. Weiner, J. (2015). The hidden costs of being an Uber driver. *Washington Post*, February 20, 2015. Available online at: https://goo.gl/wjDT0f

9. See McDermott, J. (2016). The hidden costs of driving Uber. *Mel Magazine*, March 8. Available online at: https://goo.gl/hggvje

10. Teresa Cederholm has a nice discussion of the nitty-gritty of Royal Caribbean Cruises' business model including the main categories of costs on Market Realist. It is available here: https://goo.gl/BtU7EI

11. I got these rates from reported posted by winning Priceline bidders on the chat forum BetterBidding.com. This site allows travelers to share information about their winning bids on sites such as Priceline and Hotwire so that other site users can make smart bidding decisions when using Priceline or Hotwire.

12. Available at: https://goo.gl/u4lafP

13. Available at: https://goo.gl/0hSXMq

14. See for example, Cutrone, C. (2012). Restaurant owner shows us exactly how much dishes are marked up, *Business Insider*, November 12. Available online at: https://goo.gl/uskmT7; Gordon, W. (2013). Why the hell does your drink cost so much? *Deadspin*, November 1, 2013. Available online at: https://goo.gl/p2aoUB

15. In a survey conducted by Eunsup Shim and Ephriam Sudit in the mid-1990s, the authors found that 70% of B2B companies used cost-plus pricing, and only 12% used markup pricing. See Shim, E., & Sudit, E. F. (1995). How manufacturers price products. *Strategic Finance*, 76(8), 37-39.

16. Masker, A. (2011). The downfalls of cost-plus pricing, *Profit Point Consulting*, February 16. Available online at: https://goo.gl/H5TJ5G

17. Westwood, R. (2013). What does that $14 shirt really cost? *Maclean's*, May 1. Available online at: https://goo.gl/1Tcsta

CHAPTER 5 CUSTOMER VALUE

1. Lieberman, W. H. (2012). Pricing in the cruise line industry. *Oxford Handbook of Pricing Management*. This chapter has an excellent, in-depth discus-

sion about how pricing is done in the cruise line industry. The author discusses many issues that don't have much to do with value-based pricing, but it is still a great read for anyone interested in pricing or cruise lines.

2. This issue deserves a much longer treatment than I am able to provide here. However some of the challenges with the customer value concept, and the difficulty of aligning it with financial metric's of the company's performance such as Return on Assets, profit margin, etc. are very difficult. See for example, Rust, R. T., Lemon, K. N., & Zeithaml, V. A. (2004). Return on marketing: Using customer equity to focus marketing strategy. *Journal of Marketing*, 68(1), 109-127; or Payne, A., & Frow, P. (2005). A strategic framework for customer relationship management. *Journal of Marketing*, 69(4), 167-176, for further discussion of these issues.

3. As mentioned earlier, "product" here is to be interpreted as a generic placeholder for "products and services." This is because all the concepts, ideas, and tools described apply equally well to products and services.

4. Many of these typologies are developed by consultants. In one typology that is popular at the moment, there are four categories of benefits, functional, emotional, life-changing, and social impact (see The Elements of Style" by Bain consultants Eric Almquist, John Senior, and Nicolas Bloch). In the *value pricing framework*, I avoid including abstract benefits that are hard to measure, and focus on the relatively specific functional and hedonic benefits.

5. Marketing scholars use the word "utilitarian" or "instrumental" when describing the functional benefits of the product. If I buy a hammer, for example, I expect it to be effective in driving nails into my wall. This is the core functional or utilitarian benefit provided by the hammer. Similarly, hedonic benefits refer to the positive feelings evoked by the product. For instance, when I am driving my Prius, I get a sense of fulfillment because its extreme fuel-economy matches my value of living frugally and being environmentally responsible. This is how marketing scholars Chitturi, Raghunathan, and Mahajan (2008) define these two benefits: "Consistent with previous research in marketing, we use the term "utilitarian benefits" to refer to the functional, instrumental, and practical

benefits of consumption offerings, and we use the term "hedonic benefits" to refer to their aesthetic, experiential, and enjoyment-related benefits." (p. 49). Chitturi, R., Raghunathan, R., & Mahajan, V. (2008). Delight by design: The role of hedonic versus utilitarian benefits. *Journal of Marketing*, 72(3), 48-63.

6. There is actually an organization in the Netherlands that certifies hotels by awarding them the Quiet Room label after insulating the room and making it soundproof. According to them, noisy rooms are a serious problem for generating repeat business from guests. See https://goo.gl/0Rq9YV

7. For an excellent discussion on thirty generic and widely applicable types of functional and hedonic customer value, see Almquist, E., Senior, J., & Bloch, N. (2016). The Elements of Value, *Harvard Business Review*, September. Available online at: https://goo.gl/7sFsva.

8. Dhar, R., & Wertenbroch, K. (2000). Consumer choice between hedonic and utilitarian goods. *Journal of Marketing Research*, 37(1), 60-71. In this article, the authors distinguish between products as being hedonic and utilitarian depending on their main purpose. For example, they consider a package of M&M's and a music CD as hedonic goods and a glue stick or a computer storage disk as utilitarian goods.

9. Almqust, E. (2016). The 30 things customers really value, *Harvard Business Review* digital article. Available online at: https://goo.gl/FTN4v3

10. Ramanujam, M., & Tacke, G. (2016). *Monetizing Innovation: How Smart Companies Design the Product Around the Price*, John Wiley.

11. Frei, F., & Morriss, A. (2012). *Uncommon Service: How to Win by Putting Customer at the Core of your Business*. Harvard Business School Press. The quote is from page 15.

12. The original model can be found in Emery, F. (1969). Some psychological aspects of price. In B. Taylor, & G. Wills (Eds.), *Pricing Strategy* (pp. 98-111). Staples Press. An accessible description of this model is available in Johnson, M. D. (1997), *Customer Orientation and Market Action*, New York: Prentice Hall.

13. Waber, R. L., Shiv, B., Carmon, Z., & Ariely, D. (2008). Commercial Features of Placebo and Therapeutic. *JAMA*, 299(9), 1016-1017.

CHAPTER 6 REFERENCE PRICES

1. Kalyanaram, G., & Winer, R. S. (1995). Empirical generalizations from reference price research. *Marketing Science*, 14(3), G161-G169.

2. For a review of the academic research on reference prices, see Mazumdar, T., Raj, S. P., & Sinha, I. (2005). Reference price research: Review and propositions. *Journal of Marketing*, 69(4), 84-102.

3. Garbarino, E., & Slonim, R. (2003). Interrelationships and distinct effects of internal reference prices on perceived expensiveness and demand. *Psychology & Marketing*, 20(3), 227-248.

4. Mayhew, G. E., & Winer, R. S. (1992). An empirical analysis of internal and external reference prices using scanner data. *Journal of Consumer Research*, 19(1), 62-70. This article provides excellent discussion about how shoppers use multiple reference prices when purchasing groceries in a supermarket. It provides empirical evidence to support this view.

5. Dickson, P. R., & Sawyer, A. G. (1990). The price knowledge and search of supermarket shoppers. *Journal of Marketing*, 54(3), 42-53.

6. Vanhuele, M., & Drèze, X. (2002). Measuring the price knowledge shoppers bring to the store. *Journal of Marketing*, 66(4), 72-85.

7. See Bolton, R. N., & Lemon, K. N. (1999). A dynamic model of customers' usage of services: Usage as an antecedent and consequence of satisfaction. *Journal of Marketing Research*, 171-186. This article introduces the concept of payment equity, which is the customer's evaluation of whether the prices are fair in relation to the benefits they are getting from the product. The authors call this the "evaluation of the fairness of the exchange."

8. Briesch, R. A., Krishnamurthi, L., Mazumdar, T., & Raj, S. P. (1997). A comparative analysis of reference price models. *Journal of Consumer Research*, 24(2), 202-214.

9. Kalyanaram, G., & Little, J. DC. (1994). An empirical analysis of latitude of price acceptance in consumer package goods. *Journal of Consumer Research*, 21(3), 408-418. This article covers the concept of the "latitude of price ac-

ceptance." The authors studying shopping decisions in the category of sweetened and unsweetened drinks, and find that "presence of a region of price insensitivity around a reference price." As the average reference price increases, the latitude of price acceptance also increases, meaning the customers have a wider range in which they consider the product's price to be acceptable.

10. Monroe, K. B. (1973). Buyers' subjective perceptions of price. *Journal of Marketing Research*, 10(1), 70-80.

11. Available at: https://goo.gl/BDUQ3l

12. Ratneshwar, S., Pechmann, C. & Shocker, A. D. (1996). Goal-derived categories and the antecedents of across-category consideration. *Journal of Consumer Research*, 23(3), 240-250. In this paper, the authors argue that goal-derived categories make more sense for customers in their purchase decision process. One of the examples they use is "Get a birthday present for my sister" while another was "foods that help you to cool down when you are hot." These categories may not necessarily map onto product categories as marketers tend to think of them.

13. Anderson, E. T., & Simester, D. I. (2009). Price cues and customer price knowledge. *Handbook of Pricing Research in Marketing*. Northampton, MA: Edward Elgar, 150-66.

14. Streitfield, D. (2016). An online deal just for you (Oh, and everyone else too). *New York Times*, March 6, Page A1. Available online at: https://goo.gl/5ErG8w

15. See Anderson, E. T., & Simester, D. I. (1998). The role of sale signs. *Marketing Science*, 17(2), 139-155 for a scholarly discussion of how sale signs work in price display. See Tan, S. J., & Hwang Chua, S. (2004). "While stocks last!" Impact of framing on consumers' perception of sales promotions. *Journal of Consumer Marketing*, 21(5), 343-355 for how ambiguous scarcity signs can influence consumer perceptions of prices and value.

16. Electronic Code of Federal Regulations, Title 16, Chapter 1, Subchapter B, Part 233, April 24, 2017. Available online at: https://goo.gl/BpZAjp

17. Tuttle, B. (2016). More retailers accused of misleading customers with fake price schemes. *Time*, January 7. Available online at: https://goo.gl/UGbXDJ

18. Ginzberg, E. (1936). Customary prices. *American Economic Review*, 26(2), 296-296.

19. See Balan, C. (2012). Research on Odd Prices: Dead End or Field of Potential Innovation. *Innovation in Pricing: Contemporary Theories and Best Practices*, 376-392 for a review of the academic research on this topic.

20. Anderson, E. T., & Simester, D. I. (2003). Effects of $9 price endings on retail sales: Evidence from field experiments. *Quantitative Marketing and Economics*, 1(1), 93-110.

21. Schindler, R. M., & Kirby, P. N. (1997). Patterns of rightmost digits used in advertised prices: implications for nine-ending effects. *Journal of Consumer Research*, 24(2), 192-201.

22. Simester, D. (1995). Signaling price image using advertised prices. *Marketing Science*, 14(2), 166-188.

23. Prices on the Louis Vuitton website at https:// goo.gl/FDcF7S, and for Rolex watches at swissluxury.com, https://goo.gl/sU04pH

24. Yang, S. S., Kimes, S. E., & Sessarego, M. M. (2009). $ or Dollars: Effects of Menu-price Formats on Restaurant Checks. *Cornell Hospitality Report*, 9(8), 6-11. Available online at: https://goo.gl/3PVP9c

25. Frenkel, Lior (2014). Can designers steal the best pricing techniques from restaurants? Available online at: https://goo.gl/qiYbGk

26. Dholakia, U. M., & Simonson, I. (2005). The effect of explicit reference points on consumer choice and online bidding behavior. *Marketing Science*, 24(2), 206-217.

27. Docters, R., Hanson, J., Nguyen, C., & Barzelay, M. (2012). *Contextual Pricing*, McGraw Hill, p.8.

28. Nunes, J. C., & Boatwright, P. (2004). Incidental prices and their effect on willingness to pay. *Journal of Marketing Research*, 41(4), 457-466.

CHAPTER 7 THE VALUE PROPOSITION

1. Lodish, L.M., & Mela, C. F. (2007). If brands are built over years, why are they managed over quarters? *Harvard Business Review.* Available online at: https://goo.gl/adNOlV

2. The sources for these definitions are: Kotler, P., & Keller, K. L. (2011). *Marketing Management, 14th edition*, Pearson; Capon N. (2012). *Managing Marketing in the 21st Century*, Wessex Publishing; Winer, R., & Dhar, R. (2011). *Marketing Management, 4th edition*, Prentice Hall; Osterwalder, A., Pigneur, Y., Bernada, G., & Smith, A. (2014). *Value Proposition Design: How to Create Product and Services Customers Want*, Wiley; Drews, R., & Lamson, M. (2015). *Market Entry into the USA: When European Companies Fail and How to Succeed*, Springer; Anderson, J. C, Narus, J. A., & Rossum, W. V. (2006). Customer Value Propositions in Business Markets, *Harvard Business Review*, 84, 1-4.

3. Taylor, K. (2015). The CEO of Carl's Jr. doesn't care if you're offended by the chain's sexy ads. *Entrepreneur.com*, May 20. Available online at: https://goo.gl/RDoBkv

4. W. C. Kim, & Mauborgne, R. (2004) Blue Ocean Strategy, *Harvard Business Review*, October, Available online at: https://goo.gl/McJcjg

5. Available at: https://goo.gl/7Nq3Wd

6. Available at: https://goo.gl/75WbB4

7. Brousell, L. (2015). How JetBlue uses tech to help customers take flight, *CIO Magazine*, April 17. Available online at: https://goo.gl/RIvOT5

8. Barbaro, M. (2007). Is Walmart too cheap for its own good? *New York Times*, May 30, Page C1. Available online at: https://goo.gl/HJdzm5

9. Available at: https://goo.gl/o84HMs

10. D'Aveni, R. (2010). *Beating the Commodity Trap.* Harvard Business School Press.

11. Hsieh, L. (2012). Critical issues in drilling and completions: Integrated solutions in a complex world, *Drilling Contractor Magazine*, February. Available online at: https://goo.gl/uYCMDj

12. KMBC News. Panera Bread has the most loyal customers, study finds. https://goo.gl/ZNnMXV

13. Food Business News Slide Deck. Available at: https://goo.gl/HJnE7Q

14. Available online at: https://goo.gl/n3R5AZ

15. Rothman, W. (2014). Sprint CEO Aims to Return Carrier to Its Roots: Unlimited Data Plans; Company Will Focus on Being the 'Best Value in Wireless' With Competitive Prices, *Wall Street Journal*, September 11. Available online at: https://goo.gl/4oWaLq

16. Rao, A., Bergen, M., & Davis, S. (2000). How to fight a price war. *Harvard Business Review*, March-April. Available online at: https://goo.gl/SXNW1y

17. Much of the information described in this case study is taken from one of the most transparent and detailed blog posts I have seen by Know Your Company's founder Claire Lew. It can be found here: https://goo.gl/WncnyJ

18. An excellent discussion about Salesforce.com's approach and feedback and communication mechanisms used by other companies to help senior managers, particularly CEOs obtain difficult-to-get information is provided in Gregersen, H. (2017). Bursting the CEO bubble: Why executives should talk less and ask more questions, *Harvard Business Review*, 95(2), 76-83.

19. See https://goo.gl/nBX9Z4

CHAPTER 8 PRICE EXECUTION

1. Available at: https://goo.gl/y56u9e

2. Available at: https://goo.gl/8zvpDO

3. Kalogeropoulos, D. (2015). The average American spends this much on groceries: How do you compare? *The Motley Fool*, March 7. Available online at: https://goo.gl/Mr6lIV

4. This quote is taken from Miller, J. E., & Pavesic, D. V. (1996). *Menu Pricing Strategy, Fourth Edition*, New York: John Wiley & Son.

5. Rothman, L. (2016). Putting the rising cost of college in perspective, *Time*, August 16. Available online at: https://goo.gl/b8lgzE

6. Carey, K. (2017). How colleges know what you can afford (and the limits of that tactic). *New York Times Upshot*, May 17. Available online at: https://goo.gl/NFKi8v

7. 2016 National Association of College and University Business Officers (NACUBO) Tuition Discounting Study. Available online at: https://goo.gl/JHNx82

8. CheapAir.com (2014). Airfare fluctuations: Can a flight price really change 135 times? January 21. Available online at: https://goo.gl/Q4gTS1

9. Kahn, M. (2014). Airline ticket prices shown to vary wildly among seats on the same flight. *ABC News*, August 11. Available online at: https://goo.gl/8zb198

10. The Soup Nazi refers to the episode of the television show Seinfeld of this name, in which the owner of a soup restaurant is very particular about his customers' demeanor and kicks customers out for even a slight misstep. However, his soups are so delicious that customers tolerate his insults and line up for the soup. See https://goo.gl/TW1gPh

11. Meehan, J. et al. (2011) *Pricing and profitability management: A practical guide for business leaders*, Chapter 4.

12. Monsell, J. (2016). Why Starbucks Rewards may be the most deceptive loyalty program ever, *Elliott*, June 20. Available online at: https://goo.gl/oCZpJd

13. See https://goo.gl/pocCUN

14. See Taylor, K. (2016). Customers are rebelling after Starbucks made a major change to boost profits. *Business Insider*, March 4, Available online at: https://goo.gl/YwPzfr, and Elliott, C. (2016). No Starbucks, I'm not falling for your new loyalty program. Here's why. *Elliott*. https://goo.gl/3zOlXK

15. Chakravarti, A., & Thomas, M. (2015). *Why People (Don't) Buy: The Go and Stop Signals*. Palgrave Macmillan.

16. Denning, S. (2013). J. C. Penney: Was Ron Johnson's strategy wrong? *Forbes*, April 9. Available online at: https://goo.gl/DSKfxn

17. Chace, Z. (2013). Sales are like drugs. What happens when a store wants customers to quit? *NPR Morning Edition*, March 1. Available online at: https://goo.gl/KO9r56

18. Sodhi, M., & Sodhi, N. (2008). *Six Sigma Pricing: Improving Pricing Operations to Increase Profits*, FT Press.

19. Sodhi, M., & Sodhi, N. (2005). Six sigma pricing. *Harvard Business Review*, May. Available online at: https://goo.gl/X19zUi

20. Phillips, R., Şimşek, A. S., & Van Ryzin, G. (2015). The effectiveness of field price discretion: Empirical evidence from auto lending. *Management Science*, 61(8), 1741-1759.

21. Frenzen, H., Hansen, A., Krafft, M., Mantrala, M. K., & Schmidt, S. (2010). Delegation of pricing authority to the sales force: An agency-theoretic perspective of its determinants and impact on performance. *International Journal of Research in Marketing*, 27(1), 58-68.

22. Homburg, C., Jensen, O., & Hahn, A. (2012). How to organize pricing? Vertical delegation and horizontal dispersion of pricing authority. *Journal of Marketing*, 76(5), 49-69.

23. Simon, H. (2015). *Confessions of a Pricing Man: How Price Affects Everything*. Switzerland: Springer.

CHAPTER 9 MEASURES OF PRICING SUCCESS

1. There is a vast academic literature on price promotions in consumer and business markets. See for example Mulhern, F. J., & Padgett, D. T. (1995). The relationship between retail price promotions and regular price purchases. *Journal of Marketing*, 59(4), 83-90, and Mewborn, S., Murphy, J., & Williams, G. (2014). *Clearing the roadblocks to better B2B pricing*. Bain & Company. Available online at: https://goo.gl/ntwpYa

2. The idea of satisficing is derived from Herbert Simon's work. According to him, the difference between optimizing and satisficing boils down to "looking for the sharpest needle in the haystack" (optimizing) and "looking for a needle

sharp enough to sew with" (satisficing). You can apply the same idea to pricing decisions and say you want reasonable levels of success on each of the four measures. See Simon, H. A. (1955). A behavioral model of rational choice. *The Quarterly Journal of Economics*, 69(1), 99-118.

3. Jiwoong S., & Sudhir, K. (2013). Should you punish or reward current customers? *MIT Sloan Management Review*, Fall. Available online at: https://goo.gl/HyRwCm

4. Buzzell, R. D., Gale, B. T., & Sultan, R. G. M. (1975). Market share – A key to profitability. *Harvard Business Review*, January. Available online at: https://goo.gl/LCLesf

5. See for example, Mahajan, V., Muller, E., & Bass, F. M. (1991). New product diffusion models in marketing: A review and directions for research. In *Diffusion of Technologies and Social Behavior* (pp. 125-177). Springer Berlin Heidelberg. For an excellent discussion focused on technology products, see Moore, Geoffrey A. (2009), *Crossing the Chasm: Marketing and Selling Technology Products*. Harper Collins.

6. Simon, H., Bilstein, F., & Luby, F. (2006). *Manage for Profit Not for Market Share*. Harvard Business School Press.

7. Taylor, K. (2016). Starbucks is quietly raising prices, *Business Insider*, November 21. Available online at: https://goo.gl/v6XpLB

8. Katz, B. (2016). Netflix price increase leading to 500,000 cancellations? *Forbes*, July 13. Available online at: https://goo.gl/JIXPJT

9. See for instance, Campbell, M. C. (1999). "Why did you do that?" The important role of inferred motive in perceptions of price fairness. *Journal of Product & Brand Management*, 8(2), 145-153; and Haws, K. L., & Bearden, W. O. (2006). Dynamic pricing and consumer fairness perceptions. *Journal of Consumer Research*, 33(3), 304-311.

10. Spangler, T. (2016). Netflix user sues over rate hike, claiming breach of contract. *Variety*, July 1. Available online at: https://goo.gl/zllXAw

11. Puglise, N. (2016). Prices went up at Starbucks. Did customers even notice? *The Guardian*, July 13. Available online at: https://goo.gl/bdvM6p

12. Wahba, P. (2016). Your Starbucks coffee is getting pricier today. *Fortune*, July 12. Available online at: https://goo.gl/2mDU2C

13. Namkung, Y., & Jang, S. (2017). Are consumers willing to pay more for green practices at restaurants? *Journal of Hospitality & Tourism Research*, 41(3), 329-356.

14. Greenleaf, E. A., & Lehmann, D. R. (1995). Reasons for substantial delay in consumer decision making. *Journal of Consumer Research*, 22(2), 186-199.

15. Bertini, M., & Wathieu, L. (2010). How to Stop Customers from Fixating on Price. *Harvard Business Review*, 88(5). Available at SSRN: https://goo.gl/1lvADp

16. Sandoval, G. (2012). Netflix's lost year: The inside story of the price-hike train wreck, *CNET*, July 11. Available online at: https://goo.gl/arwrhO

17. In their book, *Pricing With Confidence*, Reed Holden and Mark Burton say, "Arrogance, just a little, means that people, especially salespeople, feel confident about what their company offers and why it functions better on behalf of its customers. If they don't feel confident, how can you expect them to price with confidence?" (p. 3).

18. Truong, A. (2015). Groupon is still the fastest company to reach a billion-dollar valuation, *Quartz*, May 5. Available online at: https://goo.gl/GanIwV

19. Dholakia, U. M., What makes Groupon promotions profitable for businesses? (March 12, 2011). Available at SSRN: https://goo.gl/xxTe8K

20. Dholakia, U. M. (2011). Why employees can wreck promotional offers, *Harvard Business Review*, January-February, Available online at: https://goo.gl/YLsB2h

21. Melton, H. L., & Hartline, M. D. (2010). Customer and frontline employee influence on new service development performance. *Journal of Service Research*, 13(4), 411-425.

22. Stern, M. (2016). Starbucks leverages barista creativity to drive sales. *RetailWire*, October 20. Available online at: https://goo.gl/Eb7OeV

23. A large body of research supports this effect. See for example, Liden, R. C., Wayne, S. J., & Sparrowe, R. T. (2000). An examination of the mediating role

of psychological empowerment on the relations between the job, interpersonal relationships, and work outcomes. *Journal of Applied Psychology*, 85(3), 407-416. Also see Chen, G., Kirkman, B. L., Kanfer, R., Allen, D., & Rosen, B. (2007). A multilevel study of leadership, empowerment, and performance in teams. *Journal of Applied Psychology*, 92(2), 331-346.

24. Katzenbach, J. (2008). How to cut costs – and get your employees to help. *Strategy& White paper*. Available online at: https://goo.gl/iusCOr

25. Kiska, J. (2003). Linking employee compensation to customer feedback. *HR Professional*, January.

26. "Privately funded" means that the Indianapolis Zoo does not receive any tax support from the state or federal government. It is supported entirely by the sale of its products such as membership fees, admissions, food sales, and parking fees, and by fundraising activities through donations, grants, and events. It is still a non-profit organization.

27. Personal communication with Dennis Woerner, Director of Marketing at Indianapolis Zoo, March 7, 2017. This case study relies heavily on this interview.

28. Barbosa, D. (2014). Zoo adopts variable-pricing strategy for tickets, *Indianapolis Business Journal*, June 7. Available online at: https://goo.gl/BMbQLg

29. Available at: https://goo.gl/mWpNxx

30. I obtained these numbers from the Indianapolis Zoo's annual reports available here: https://goo.gl/PdCYPI

31. Verbatim comments of Dennis Woerner, Director of Marketing at Indianapolis Zoo, personal interview conducted on March 7, 2017.

CHAPTER 10 PRICING BUSINESS PRODUCTS

1. See Hinterhuber, A. (2008). Customer value-based pricing strategies: why companies resist. *Journal of Business Strategy*, 29(4), 41-50. In it, the author discusses the bullish opinions of various experts about the superiority of value-based pricing in detail.

2. A classic article on this topic is Bagozzi, R. P. (1975). Marketing as exchange. *Journal of Marketing*, 39, 32-39.

3. Customer types in a business market correspond closely to customer segments in consumer markets. We do want to make the distinction here to acknowledge the fact that the customers of one particular type closely interact with each other, and reference each other explicitly in their buying decisions. There is very little referencing across customer types. In the oil-field services, a small independent oil exploration and development company would see itself as completely different from a major producer like Exxon Mobil and wouldn't care much about Exxon's buying processes or how it derives value. We can think of each customer type as a fairly self-contained group of similar customers who can be treated as identical for the purposes of value pricing.

4. Available at: https://goo.gl/kvMiWM

5. Available at: https://goo.gl/Sr9npV

6. Details about the drug can be found on Pfizer's website: https://goo.gl/zVhmrW

7. Rockoff, J. (2015). How Pfizer set the cost of its new drug at $9.850 a month. *Wall Street Journal*, December 9. Available online at: https://goo.gl/1cHJM8

8. Available at: https://goo.gl/p6xdkd

9. Available at: https://goo.gl/M82usY

10. Siddiqui, M. & Rajkumar, S. V. (2012). The high cost of cancer drugs and what we can do about it. *Mayo Clinic Proceedings*, 87(10), 935-943. Available online at: https://goo.gl/JULicf

CHAPTER 11 PRICING CONSUMER PRODUCTS

1. Shapiro, C., & Varian, H. R. (1998). Versioning: the smart way to sell information. *Harvard Business Review*, 107(6), 106-114. Available online at: https://goo.gl/hzP6d5

2. Dholakia, U. M. (2000). Temptation and resistance: an integrated model of consumption impulse formation and enactment. *Psychology & Marketing*, 17(11), 955-982.

3. Wood, W., & Neal, D. T. (2009). The habitual consumer. *Journal of Consumer Psychology*, 19(4), 579-592.

4. Kahn, B. E., & Isen, A. M. (1993). The influence of positive affect on variety seeking among safe, enjoyable products. *Journal of Consumer Research*, 20(2), 257-270.

5. Chernev, A. (2006). Differentiation and Parity in assortment pricing. *Journal of Consumer Research*, 33(2), 199-210.

6. Dudlicek, J. (2015). Stack the meat case with value and simplicity, *Progressive Grocer*, November 25. Available online at: https://goo.gl/r8t6al

7. See Peck, J., & Childers, T. L. (2006). If I touch it I have to have it: Individual and environmental influences on impulse purchasing. *Journal of Business Research*, 59(6), 765-769.

8. Available at: https://goo.gl/h4puhx

9. Mohammed, R. (2013). Why good-better-best prices are so effective, *Harvard Business Review*, February 8. Available online at: https://goo.gl/xC4ocn

10. Farley, A. (2014). Is premium economy worth it? *Travel & Leisure Magazine*, June 9. Available online at: https://goo.gl/iWIiss

11. Michaels, D. (2014). Why this plane seat is the most profitable. *Wall Street Journal*, March 4. Available online at: https://goo.gl/wmX0Cp

12. Available at: https://goo.gl/4ctfrd

13. Williams, G. C. (2016). Chrysler redesigns, cuts minivan line down to single model for 2017. *Houston Chronicle*, August 11. Available online at: https://goo.gl/2Ufz9F

14. Egan, J. (2014). Storage war: What happens to your stuff when you don't pay your self-storage rent? *Huffington Post*, July 24. Available online at: https://goo.gl/V8kRWc

15. Gallego, G., & Stefanescu, C. (2012). *Services engineering: Design and pricing of service features.* Chapter 28 of the Oxford Handbook of Pricing Management. Oxford, UK: Oxford University Press.

16. Budd, A. (2007). Opera vs. Microsoft. Available online at: https://goo.gl/fFtBIU

17. Avorn, J. (2005). Torcetrapib and atorvastatin-should marketing drive the research agenda? *New England Journal of Medicine*, 352(25), 2573-76.

18. Quigley, E. (2017). How you get tickets to see Hamilton in Austin. *Austin360*, February 24. Available online at: https://goo.gl/jeZPHj

19. Segran, E. (2015). From socks to sex toys: Inside America's subscription-box obsession, *Fast Company*, April 6. Available online at: https://goo.gl/7H53Wl

20. Lake, L. (2016). Extra! Extra! Read all about the subscription deception, Federal Trade Commission Consumer Information. Available online at: https://goo.gl/La2M2J

21. Vigna, S. D., & Malmendier, U. (2006). Paying not to go to the gym. *American Economic Review*, 96(3), 694-719.

ABOUT THE AUTHOR

Utpal Dholakia is a professor of marketing and holds the George R. Brown Chair of Marketing at Rice University in Houston, Texas. He teaches marketing and pricing strategies to MBA students, and conducts research on consumer behavior & welfare, digital marketing, and marketing strategy issues.

His research has been published in the top marketing and management journals and has been cited extensively. He has consulted and provided expert witness services to many financial services, technology, healthcare, and energy companies.

Utpal's popular blog on Psychology Today is called *The Science Behind Behavior*. You can learn more about him and his work, and connect with him at **utpaldholakia.com**.

Made in the USA
San Bernardino, CA
21 October 2017